"Ten lawyers representing ... Dallas' top family law litigation firms got together ... and decided to make divorce clients a promise: If you want to walk away from your marriage without a bloody battle ... we will put down our litigators' guns and help you do it."

Texas Bar Journal, March 2000

"Texas' reputation for rough-and-tumble justice may be in for a revision ... the state became the first in the nation to adopt a statute clearing the way for collaborative law, a process designed to soften the experience of getting a divorce."

ABA Journal, March 2002

"It's the sense of control that is so much better in collaborative law. Instead of lawyers and judges being in control, the control remains very firmly with the husband and wife."

The Dallas Morning News, September 2002

Divorce Without Disaster

Collaborative Law in Texas

Janet P. Brumley
Collaborative Family Lawyer

Published by PSG Books
Dallas, Texas

Divorce Without Disaster
Collaborative Law in Texas

By Janet P. Brumley

PSG Books
9830 Kingsley Road, No. 405
Dallas, Texas 75238
(214) 340-6223   fax (214) 343-9063
info@prosolutionsgroup.com

Books published under the imprint of PSG Books are distributed to the U.S. book trade by Independent Publishers' Group, 814 N. Franklin St., Chicago, Illinois 60610. Resellers outside the book trade who wish to purchase books in quantity at a discount may contact PSG Books toll-free at (800) 465-1508.

Attorney and author Janet P. Brumley is available to speak to groups on the subject of divorce and the pressing need for the collaborative law process. She can be reached at the law firm of Verner & Brumley, P.C., 3131 Turtle Creek Blvd., Dallas, Texas 75219, (214) 526-5234, or by e-mail: jbrumley@vernerbrumley.com.

ISBN 0-9659273-7-7

Manufactured in the United States of America

9 8 7 6 5 4 3 2 1

Library of Congress Cataloging-in-Publication Data

Brumley, Janet P., 1950-
Divorce without disaster: collaborative law in Texas/
by Janet P. Brumley.
p. cm.
ISBN 0-9659273-7-7
1. Divorce suits — Texas. 2. Dispute resolution (Law) —
Texas. I. Title.
KFT1300.B78 2004
346.76401'66 — dc22
2003020286

NOTICE AND DISCLAIMER

State laws, legal precedents and regulations vary greatly from one jurisdiction to another and change over time. Because of these variations, the reader should not use this book for specific legal advice. Every divorce case and post-divorce action is unique, requiring the advice of those versed in the laws of the jurisdiction where the action is taken at the time it is taken.

This book is intended to provide readers with a general overview of matters related to the divorce process and post-divorce issues, so they may take legal action or otherwise address these issues better informed. Consult an attorney for specific information related to your personal situation.

PUBLISHER'S NOTE

Janet P. Brumley's book, *Divorce Without Disaster: Collaborative Law in Texas,* is the first in a series on this new method of marital dissolution.

Working with outstanding authors such as Brumley, PSG Books is committed to providing information on collaborative law to divorcing people, attorneys and other professionals in as many states as possible over the next few years. This new series follows our *Successful Divorce* books and State Financial Divorce Guides.

Collaborative law practitioners interested in co-authoring editions in this series for their states should contact:

PSG Books
9830 Kingsley Road, No. 405
Dallas, Texas 75238
Attention: Larry Upshaw
(214) 340-6223
E-mail: info@prosolutionsgroup.com

ABOUT THE AUTHOR

Janet P. Brumley has more than 25 years' experience as a divorce lawyer. During that time, she has gained a reputation as a fierce advocate on behalf of her clients in the domestic relations courts of Texas. Janet is board certified in family law by the Texas Board of Legal Specialization and is a member of the College of the State Bar of Texas.

In 2003, she was selected one of the Texas Super Lawyers through a poll of other lawyers published by *Texas Monthly* and *Law & Politics* magazines.

In the last few years, Janet has found a more civil way to obtain the best possible result for those who retain her. She is a certified mediator and a member of both the International Academy of Collaborative Professionals and the Collaborative Law Institute of Texas. She is also a founding member of the Dallas Alliance of Collaborative Family Lawyers, a group of attorneys from different law firms whose common thread is their dedication to the sane and sensible features of collaborative law divorce.

Janet earned her law degree from the University of Memphis School of Law. She has served on the grievance committee of the State Bar of Texas and she often teaches at continuing legal education seminars for the State Bar. This includes presenting at the Advanced Family Law Course, the largest gathering of family lawyers in the nation.

Janet concentrates her practice on collaborative law.

— Publisher

ACKNOWLEDGMENTS

I would like to thank Minnesota attorney Stuart Webb for inventing this beautiful process. I would also like to thank Pauline Tesler and Chip Rose, along with Stu Webb, for their thorough, professional and inspiring training that was essential to my becoming a collaborative law practitioner. Hundreds of attorneys across the country have undergone their training in the last few years, and people who divorce under collaborative law principles have these fine teachers to thank for a less-painful outcome.

This book would not exist without the indulgence and wise counsel of my law partners, Jimmy Verner and Paul Brumley. Jimmy has extensive experience writing about legal topics, and he helped me set a tone that I hope you feel is right for you and all people looking at the possibility of a collaborative law divorce. Since Paul is also my partner in life, he tolerated numerous evenings and weekends when I was too "booked" in front of the computer to be a good companion.

A special thank-you goes out to PSG Books editor Lori Fairchild and publisher Larry Upshaw. They worked diligently to help me transform my thoughts and ideas into the book you are holding now.

And I extend my gratitude and respect to my fellow members of the Dallas Alliance of Collaborative Family Lawyers, the first collaborative law practice group in the state of Texas. They have shared their knowledge, opinions, feelings and support for the three years since we formed the Alliance. Their biographies are at the back of this book along with a listing of all the other great Texas attorneys who are trained in collaborative law.

— Janet P. Brumley

TABLE OF CONTENTS

Introduction

INTRODUCTION

Litigation was my life for the first 22 years of my practice. Like most litigators, I thought the opposition needed a swift kick sometimes, and I was the one to administer it. From the time I was a child on the playground, if someone was mistreated, it was my job to make things right.

There is something righteous and intoxicating about fighting for someone else. I loved to tell someone who was scared and lonely (as all divorcing parties are) that I would protect them. Each time I've been appointed a guardian ad litem for children, I've introduced myself by saying that I am a cross between a guardian angel and a guard dog. I work for them and will protect them from all harm. It's more than intoxicating. It's mother's milk.

I went into law for the joy of being this protector. I've heard criminal attorneys convince themselves that they are protecting the Constitution. I suppose attorneys who defend large corporations believe they are doing God's work, too.

But there came a time about three years ago when I realized the avenging angel who only does good is a delusion. How could this be? I *had* to be doing right when my clients told me they didn't know what they would do without me.

I enjoyed what I was hearing, but not what I was seeing. What I thought was fixed kept coming unfixed. I would win a custody trial only to be back in court a couple of years later fighting modification of the custody order.

You see, in family law litigation, winning only sets you up to lose. The person who wins thinks this is the end of the story. But just as no war has ever left the world a peaceful place, these divorce wars are only a precursor of battles to come. The supposed loser in the battle simply lies in wait to prove he or she was wronged. Nothing gets resolved. The parties' anger gets validated to the point that they can hardly stand to look at each other, much less work together for the good of children or themselves.

Finding collaborative law was an epiphany for me. Finally, a process encourages people to be reasonable, even when they don't want to be. Everyone can't leave the chaos behind and approach the future with new resolve. But they have a much better chance of accomplishing that with collaborative law than with litigation or even mediation. Plus, they get to keep their privacy and dignity intact.

The downside for the attorney is that in collaborative law, you are literally replaceable. Your participation agreement clearly states that if settlement fails, another attorney will replace you. But there's an upside for the attorney, too. The opposing party doesn't despise you. For each client who absolutely loved me, there was a spouse on the other side who hated the sight of me.

Now everyone in this process sees me for what I am — another mortal who knows Texas family law and is trying to help them help themselves. I am no longer the know-all, end-all and be-all, but I am also not the snake. Attorneys engaged in the process empower the parties to make good decisions and solidify their own futures.

That makes me proud of what I do today. I don't see myself reflected in anyone's mirror but my own. And I see those days on the schoolyard more clearly. Pulling that big-mouthed kid off the see-saw for calling people names didn't solve anything. It only caused the kid at the other end of the board to hit the ground as collateral damage.

— Janet P. Brumley

*This book is dedicated
with love to Jason, Jessica
and Laura Elizabeth*

What Is Collaborative Law and Why Use It?

Every divorce begins with a love story and ends in disappointment. A man and a woman are overcome by sadness and hurt. They have feelings of misplaced trust. They often regret the years they feel were lost and mourn for a future they won't have together. If children are involved, the hurt is magnified by feelings of guilt.

How sad that we make the situation worse by the divorce process itself. There is every reason to make the situation better by using a process that is healing and restorative rather than destructive and alienating.

Parties to divorce in Texas often use the legal system as a means of getting even for real or imagined wrongs committed during the marriage. Revenge is popular. The community estate and the children of the marriage are often destroyed as a byproduct of a hazy bit of temporary insanity that seems to grip people when they surrender themselves to the power of the court system.

A decade ago, judges and attorneys tried to mitigate the effects of family law litigation by insisting in as many jurisdictions as possible that parties submit to mediation before going to court. This form of alternative dispute resolution is either required or strongly encouraged in most big-city family courts in Texas, and that has helped. But sometimes mediation is just a way station en route to the courthouse. What the system needed was a method of marital dissolution that opted people out of the court system entirely.

Texas Divorces Involve Two Different Rulebooks

Today, the Texas legal system handles divorces under one of two different sets of rules:

(1) The traditional method begins with filing, then moves to discovery, temporary orders, hearings and attempted alternative dispute resolution, or mediation. This entire process is controlled from the courthouse, under the Rules of Civil Procedure, and is referred to as litigation.

(2) The non-traditional method occurs outside the courthouse and the Rules of Civil Procedure, and is handled in a private forum known as collaborative law.

Choices of How to End the Marriage

From the vantage point of the divorcing parties, there are many methods based on the amount of cooperation couples must exhibit and how much outside help they need to resolve their disagreements.

Kitchen Table Approach – This is direct negotiation between the parties. It can work well if the parties are at a high-functioning point in their lives and can communicate with each other. You rarely find this during a divorce. If the parties can approach each other on an even footing, this is the most efficient and productive way to end a marriage. If not, this method allows for the domination, manipulation and coercion that frequently accompany the breakdown of a relationship.

Negotiation of Terms with a Therapist – This is pure mediation, even though the therapist may not be trained in mediation techniques. This method does not subject you to the legal system, but it also does not give you the benefit of legal advice. Parties frequently make agreements that are not enforceable in courts of law or omit issues that must be addressed in a divorce decree.

Collaborative Law – This involves open communication among both spouses and their attorneys. It allows for the parties to make agreements on all the issues that need to be addressed and makes certain such agreements are enforceable. It is true conflict resolution.

Mediation – This is done in a caucus or shuttle style. Agreements are frequently obtained on all issues in a form that is enforceable. It requires three attorneys — one for each party and one to act as mediator. Mediation usually takes place after a temporary orders hearing and after discovery is complete. Mediation is designed as the step just before a full trial.

Special Master/Arbitrator – This is a hearing before a private judge. You can get a speedier hearing this way than at the courthouse, in a setting that is more private and convenient than court. Nothing is *resolved* here, only ended.

Litigation – This is the most public, intrusive, damaging avenue for divorce. However, it does end the marriage and sometimes it is the only way that works for the situation and the parties involved.

Janet P. Brumley

A Closer Look at Collaborative Law

The core principle of collaborative law is that each attorney and each party to the divorce pledges to sit down across from each other in the same room and pursue settlement of the case in the most cooperative way possible, without guns, venom or a roadmap to disaster. They vow to keep talking until they reach settlement, and to stay out of court at all cost.

It took an unassuming Minnesota family attorney named Stuart Webb to create collaborative law. Back in 1990, he became disenchanted with the outcomes he was seeing and announced that he no longer would take a divorce into the courtroom. To his competitors, Webb's move was unilateral disarmament. Clients wondered at first if this was a serious way to approach a divorce. To Webb, it was just the natural next step in a process that was heading into alternate methods of dispute resolution.

Collaborative law divorces are becoming commonplace in a growing number of states as more attorneys seek collaborative law training and the word spreads about the benefits of this process.

"My estimate is that collaborative law is alive and well in 30 states and six Canadian provinces," says Webb. "There are about 3,500 collaborative lawyers, and more are going through the training each day."

But it's impossible, he contends, to specify the number of divorces being done collaboratively in North America. Not all collaborative lawyers have been as closely tied to this method as he is. Some handle a collaborative law case one day, mediation the next. And some still litigate divorces in a small number of cases.

Collaborative Law Can Save Everything

The most commonly asked question is "What does this type of divorce save you?" People catch on to the idea that a divorce under collaborative law can save you money. That's not always the case. But a survey in *American Lawyer* magazine estimated the average attorney fees in a collaborative law case are about one-third the amount of a litigated divorce.

Money is only one thing you save. Pursuing divorce collaboratively can save you everything — time, your children's self-esteem, friendships, privacy, assets and whatever relationship you have left with your spouse.

Doing your divorce collaboratively is much like getting a hand-tailored suit instead of one off the rack. A litigated divorce follows a predictable pattern fitted to the needs of legal professionals, not to your needs.

A collaborative divorce, on the other hand, fits the particular needs of your family. An off-the-rack suit almost fits you, but the pants may be a little tight across the pockets and a little long. The tailored pants fit perfectly, and that makes all the difference in how you feel about them.

Of course, in the real-life version of my metaphor, the hand-tailored suit always costs more than the others. To make the metaphor work, you have to imagine the hand-tailored suit made of an attractive and durable fabric that costs no more (in fact, probably less) than the off-the-rack suit. Would you really let the salesperson talk you into buying the off-the-rack suit or would you insist on the better product?

Collaborative law removes control of the divorce process from judges, juries and attorneys and gives it to the parties, where it belongs. Throughout this book, I relate experiences and give you examples of how truly revolutionary collaborative law is, and how beneficial it is for everyone involved.

But none of this information about collaborative law is as powerful as the following exchange between two people who divorced through the collaborative process. Ken and Abbe Hitchcock were married for 18 years and have three children. What's remarkable is that both of them consented to being quoted about their divorce in the same book. Most survivors of litigated divorces can't stand to be in the same room together. In most cases, the level of suspicion is so high that if I were to ask one side to comment, the other side would naturally not want to be quoted.

"We came out of it much better than we would have if somebody had told us what we were going to do," says Ken Hitchcock. "Civility was the key. Because we had an agenda and a goal for each meeting, we were both able to be civil. It forced a lot of interaction between us because we had to make decisions on our own. We made every decision based on mutual agreement, and nobody left angry. I've been told by people who have heard about this process it's unbelievable that we were able to handle it like that."

Abbe Hitchcock adds: "You often hear about people using negative tactics during a divorce, but in my opinion, that can have a lifelong negative impact on the family and is simply unnecessary. Behaving that way would not only have reflected poorly on me, but it also would have hurt my children. I saw firsthand how hurtful a traditional, adversarial divorce was for the children of a good friend of mine, and I just wanted a process that was going to take care of me and my children, in the least hostile manner.

What Is Collaborative Law?

"Divorce is difficult for anybody," she continues, "but this process was much smoother and left us feeling we had more control of our destination. It can be very painful, but it's much better when you're sitting down together with both of your attorneys and working this out together rather than in a courtroom where somebody else is going to tell you how you're going to live your life and when you're going to see your children."

Human Behavior Key to Collaborative Law

The need for people to participate in major decision-making during a crucial period of life is at the root of this move to collaborative law. Just as medicine is evolving away from the physician giving the patient orders and toward more interaction between the doctor and the patient, participation is growing between the lawyer and the client. Today, patients want to know which medicines and procedures can help them recover and consider the pros and cons of each. People contemplating divorce want to know which legal processes best fit their situation, so they can, with an attorney's advice, choose for themselves.

For most people, the collaborative law process is an attractive one that can prove effective. We want to control our lives and decisions, as long as we feel safe doing so. Collaborative law allows us to create a safe environment and achieve good results. The attorneys act as a safety net for the parties. The parties each know that the attorneys will jump in if they are about to make an agreement that is unenforceable or unwise.

Attorneys untrained in collaborative law often claim that it can't work, that people are much too vindictive or stupid or mean to allow the process to work, especially in family law matters. This simply is incorrect.

"The divorce model of the past has involved, at times, intense litigation and conflict, which prevented families from moving forward with positive momentum," says Patrick A. Savage, a psychotherapist and mediator who was one of the first therapists in Dallas to work on collaborative law divorces. "I have trained with attorneys who are learning to move from an adversarial approach to one of collaboration in order to perform the helpful services they can provide as 'counselors at law.' I have seen collaborative attorneys assist their clients in resolving conflicts to find closure by the end of the divorce.

"Using the collaborative process helps the couple understand their role in the divorce, better problem-solve, explore the best interests of the entire family, co-parent their children and move into new relationships without the continued baggage from the previous marriage," Savage adds.

Collaboration, he points out, is an extreme team effort that puts all the information on the table early, so the pieces are there to work with. "What's happening is, instead of the attorney saying, 'The other side wants this; don't give it to them,' the attorney asks, 'What is in the best interest of these clients and their children?'"

We know it's much easier for people to do harm to others if they can do it from far away and are not engaged with that person. It's infinitely easier for pilots to bomb a village from several thousand feet in the air than it is for soldiers to attack when they see children playing in the streets. If you put people in a room across from each other, most will back off their desire to do harm and instead will do right.

Simple proximity can have this amazing effect. Coming

face to face with the opposition, the vast majority of people will defuse whatever bombs they may be carrying, saving themselves as well as the *enemy*. The process of collaborative law is like that. It helps clients and attorneys evolve from their lower-functioning isolated selves into higher-functioning integrated people.

Who Can Use Collaborative Law?

Once you understand collaborative law and appreciate what it can accomplish, it's important to determine if you will benefit from a divorce using this process.

Collaborative law is a worthwhile alternative for divorcing couples who want to speak to each other after the divorce. It is for those who want no negative baggage left with the other side once the divorce is final. The process is especially sound for anyone with children.

But collaborative law is not appropriate in every case. It usually doesn't work if there has been a history of domestic violence in the marriage. In those cases, the victim is often emotionally battered and unable to be in the same room with the abuser and think clearly at the same time. Also, the abuser knows subtle ways of conveying terror in the victim that go unrecognized by the attorneys for both parties.

Collaborative law should be viewed skeptically in marriages where either party has an untreated or unacknowledged substance abuse or mental problem. People under the influence may make agreements they don't understand and never intend to honor. Collaborative law requires two whole, thinking persons who are capable of stepping outside their anger and hurt, and acting rationally.

That does not mean angry or hurt people cannot

employ collaborative law. On the contrary, almost every divorcing person is angry and hurt.

The collaborative process is conflict resolution, not conflict-free resolution. But it requires the ability and willingness to value other things more than revenge, such as the well-being of children, the continued ability to co-parent or the ability to see the ex-spouse in the workplace or socially without rancor.

Effective Collaborative Law Participants:

... want to protect everything — children, relationships, money, time and privacy.

... tend to be intelligent and educated, and have a higher-than-average emotional IQ.

... want a divorce that is "tailor-made" for their circumstances, not an "off-the- rack," ill-fitting form used by everyone (and fitting no one very well).

... want results more than revenge.

... want to be participants — not victims — in the dissolution of the marriage.

... want to assure themselves that nothing happens unless they agree to it.

... want some control over the scheduling of events of divorce.

... want to retain some dignity through the process of divorce.

... want to end the relationship as positively as possible.

... see the big picture.

2 What Makes Collaborative Law Different from Litigation?

B elow are some specific features that distinguish collaborative law from litigation.

Communication

In litigation, communication is limited and frequently destructive.

In collaborative law, the parties and their attorneys communicate openly and constructively.

Use of Expert Testimony

In litigation, each side employs its own experts. That frequently results in the parties paying two bills, and the court may ignore both experts as biased.

In collaborative law, the parties and attorneys agree on a single expert in a particular field (home appraiser, financial advisor, therapist) and pay the expert from the community estate, resulting in less expense and more truth.

Privacy

In litigation, testimony becomes a matter of public record.

In collaborative law, everything is conducted in private joint sessions that are neither transcribed nor public.

Scheduling

In litigation, all events (depositions, hearings, etc.) are scheduled with no consideration of the parties' schedules, or to inconvenience the other party.

In collaborative law, the parties schedule everything themselves, with their attorneys present.

Speed of Resolution

In litigation, each case moves at the speed of the attorneys and court.

In collaborative law, each case moves at the speed of the parties.

Redemptive Resolution of Conflict

In litigation, each party gets to "slap" the other one multiple times. Usually, having the opportunity to beat up on the other side makes an anguished person feel better, at least momentarily, but nothing ever gets resolved. At some point, the legal process merely ends.

In collaborative law, the attorneys help the parties resolve issues, so resentment and anger are defused rather than merely deflected. Everybody wants to think well of themselves and be thought of the same way by others. Even in the midst of hurt, anger and anguish, most collaborative law participants keep their heads, behave and do right by themselves and their spouses.

More on Communication

In a standard litigation divorce, the parties are instructed not to speak to each other directly about the case, but to talk only through attorneys. There is a good reason for this admonition. Usually tempers are short and parties are not operating at their highest level. This results in lower functioning than at most other times in their lives.

A person going through a divorce is stressed and hurt, and may not hear well or communicate effectively. It is a recipe for disaster for two angry and hurt people to try to talk substantively with no assistance. What generally happens is that the two people sit down to civilly discuss their problems and possible solutions. At first, they do well and make some progress. Sooner or later, though, one of them takes a potshot at the other (or at least that's how it is perceived) and the fight is on. When they finish, they've not only lost all the progress they made, but they've actually dug themselves into a more negative position than where they started.

Collaborative attorneys are trained to actively listen. When either attorney hears a distracting comment by the parties, he or she will use a method designed to get the conversation back on track. Collaborative attorneys prefer to do a collaborative case with another collaboratively trained attorney, rather than with an attorney who is not trained in the model.

It has been my experience that if the other attorney is untrained, but is a cooperative person with whom I have handled prior cases and built up a mutual trust, the collaborative divorce can proceed smoothly. In this situation, I will have to do most of the work — not because the other lawyer isn't willing, but because he or she doesn't know what needs to be done. If the other attorney is not particularly cooperative and is untrained in collaborative law, using the collaborative process can be difficult because so much time is spent overcoming the other attorney's aggressive attitude.

Referring back to my analogy of the hand-tailored versus off-the-rack suit, the untrained lawyer keeps trying to convince everyone it's fine that the suit is too tight and the pockets stick out. That lawyer doesn't understand why everyone won't just shut up and take the suit!

Further, in a standard litigation divorce, attorneys are prohibited from speaking directly to the client on the other side. A paradigm in which discourse is limited is not as effective as one in which everyone talks to everyone else.

Litigation Communication

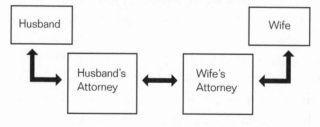

Collaborative Law Communication

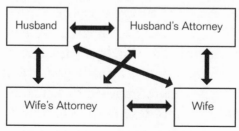

"One of the very frustrating things that frequently happens in litigation is that no one is talking to each other. The clients aren't talking directly to each other, and sometimes the lawyers aren't even talking to one another," explains Paula Larsen, a member of the Dallas Alliance of Collaborative Family Lawyers and a partner in the Dallas-based firm of Goranson Bain & Larsen.

"Your client calls and tells you something, then you call the other lawyer. If you're lucky, you can get him or her, or maybe you have to talk to the legal assistant. It's like the telephone game, and by the time you get to the end of the line, who knows what's been translated to the client? There are so many opportunities for confusion."

"But in a collaborative context," Larsen continues, "because everyone is there together, there just is not nearly the opportunity for the kind of confusion or poor communication that's built into the litigation model. In 23 years as an attorney, I have never seen litigation improve parties' communication."

Some clients report that their strained communication was strengthened and improved as a result of the collaborative process. "It wasn't an easy thing, because there are a lot of raw feelings involved, but I think that having the four parties — the two of us and our lawyers — sitting down together in a process that fosters communication, was very helpful," says Andy Chaffin, a Dallas CPA who was divorced in 2000. "We have two children in college now, so we're still dealing with those kinds of parenting issues and I think our communication has actually gotten better. Using the collaborative process as opposed to something perhaps more damaging emotionally allowed us to have better communication going forward. If you're going to have any kind of relationship down the road with the person you're divorcing, this process can assist in building communication skills that you can use later."

Use of Expert Testimony

Frequently in divorce, the parties need help from outside experts. The parties may disagree over the fair market value of their residence and need an appraiser to determine that value. Or they may disagree on a child's medication and need the advice of a pediatrician. In more complicated divorces, there may be questions of tracing separate property, valuing the couple's interest in a trust or determining the value of a business. In each instance, the attorney for each party in a litigation divorce hires an expert to give his or her opinion to the court in the final trial. These experts realize they have been hired by one interested party and, therefore, may give an opinion that benefits that party.

This nefarious lack of integrity is not universal, but it does occur. Most lawyers who practice family law know the local experts who cannot be bought and will give their honest, professional opinion without bias. These are the experts hired in collaborative law cases. Unlike the two-expert duel in litigation, in collaborative law the parties and attorneys agree on one expert and pay the expert from the community estate.

"It's a lot easier to appraise a property, and get all the important variables that are involved, when both sides are in agreement with you being there," says real estate appraiser D.W. Skelton. "When you're hired by only one side, the other side sometimes thinks you're going to give a higher or lower valuation based on what your side wants. They're constantly worried about that, and they may make it difficult for the appraiser to get into the home to do what he needs to do, such as take photographs or make notes. If the parties are civil to each other, no matter what type of divorce it is, you don't run into any of that."

This also applies to the mental-health experts often called on during a divorce process. "With collaborative law, I'm hired by both attorneys, so it's clear that I have the best interest of the relationship and the family in mind," says therapist Patrick Savage. "Since there's no other therapist involved, I'm able to render an opinion that both attorneys will honor, since it's not about winning or losing; it's about what's in their clients' best interest."

More on Privacy

When litigants go to the courthouse for a hearing or an attorney's office for a deposition or witness statement, proceedings are usually on the record. People who value privacy are suddenly in an open courtroom discussing their sex lives, their finances and their taxes. This is all recorded by a court reporter and saved for posterity. Inventories and appraisements listing all the parties' assets and liabilities (complete with account numbers) are routinely filed with the district clerk of their county of residence.

Parties who resolve their divorces with collaborative law do so behind closed doors in their attorneys' offices. The law prohibits attorneys from disclosing anything they have heard, except in cases where someone declares an intent to commit a crime or poses a continuing threat of child abuse.

"Collaborative law is a cooperative effort, not a public forum," observes Mary Jo McCurley, a partner in the Dallas firm of McCurley Orsinger McCurley & Nelson and chair of the family law section of the State Bar of Texas. "With collaborative law, you can settle the case with a scalpel rather than a hatchet, which is what you get in court. Because the parties have crafted the agreement themselves, they own it more than if a judge has told them what to do. They're more likely to follow the terms of the agreement."

Scheduling and Speed of Resolution

Most courts have an interest in maintaining control of their docket, which is the list of cases due for trial. Some judges like to move things along faster than the parties prefer. With other judges, you have to wait for a hearing and the case languishes. In litigation, the parties have no control over the scheduling and timing of events. Attorneys have a small amount of control over things like depositions, but frequently they use this control for bad rather than good. For instance, a deposition might be scheduled purposely to inconvenience the other party.

Zealous representation and advocacy by an attorney can be a destructive thing in litigation. The attorney may identify so closely with the client that the attorney wants to "hurt" the spouse who hurt his or her client. "They become so focused on winning that they miss the point of helping their client, and somebody is guaranteed to come out in bad shape," says therapist Savage.

Clients usually get a great deal of comfort from these actions and may encourage the behavior. It is understandable from the litigant's perspective, because he or she is feeling beleaguered and alone. The adage "The enemy of my enemy is my friend," often takes over.

Of course, if you hit someone where it hurts, that person usually will strike back where it hurts you the most. Then you need to hit again, and on and on. Before you know it, the case has dragged on for years and cost you tens of thousands of dollars in experts' and attorneys' fees and even more in lost revenue from inconvenient scheduling.

In collaborative law, each party works to resolve certain problems and finalize the divorce, maximizing the retention of assets.

Which Method Resolves Conflict

There's a story by country comedian Jerry Clower that goes something like this:

A man found himself treed with a mountain lion. He and the mountain lion were fighting to the death. His friend on the ground had the only gun but was afraid to shoot for fear of hitting his compatriot. The man in the tree spent some time wrestling with the mountain lion and yelling to his friend to shoot the animal, to no avail. The friend was afraid he'd shoot the man instead of the mountain lion, but the man in the tree finally shouted to his friend, "Just shoot! One of us has got to get some relief!"

That's how it goes at the courthouse. Each party puts on his or her witnesses and the judge takes out one of his or her judicial weapons and shoots down somebody's legal case. Usually one party perceives himself or herself to be the loser. That person now has a cause. For the rest of time, the loser will try to get even with the winner, if only in that person's own mind.

The fight does not end at the courthouse door when the divorce is final. It goes on and on. People remember who testified for them and who spoke against them. There is a reckoning for all those friends and family members who, bless their hearts, probably didn't even want to be involved. The party who perceives himself or herself to be the winner feels vindicated and believes the whole bloody mess is over. No one understands why it isn't.

But divorce lawyers and preachers and psychologists know it isn't over, and they know why — because the underlying problems are not resolved. Neither party gets to speak and be heard and validated by the other. Just as the parties can't be married effectively, neither can they divorce effectively. They continue to carry their hurt and resentment and anger. If they believe they won, they take it as a declaration of their total innocence and lack of fault. If they believe they lost, they feel misunderstood and victimized yet again. Neither of these positions is a good foundation for a future.

In collaborative law, instead of agreeing with the damaging and hurtful, but completely understandable, assertions of the "injured" spouse, the attorney helps to reframe the perspective to a healthier one. Instead of allowing the client to become obsessed with the details of keeping score, the collaborative attorney helps the client see the larger picture and focus on more meaningful matters. It is more difficult work than being a litigator, but also more fulfilling.

"People generally demonstrate more respect for one another in the collaborative setting," says Donald R. Royall, partner in The Royalls, a Houston family law firm, and past chair of the family law section of the State Bar of Texas. "An important factor is the opportunity for mentoring that this process affords for the lawyers. Contrary to the courtroom setting, the lawyers are not expected to be confrontational in collaboration, even when they disagree. They can model appropriate behavior without being concerned that they might not be living up to their client's expectations of their skills as a courtroom advocate."

As one of the parties to the divorce, you don't have to remain married to your difficult spouse, but you don't get to beat him or her to a bloody pulp, either. From the perspective of interest-based negotiation, this is good for you because if you don't try to administer a beating, then there's no need for your opponent to return the favor.

Theodore Roosevelt was the first major world leader to embrace the notion of mediating conflict between nations by encouraging dialogue. Naysayers hissed "It will never work. Why is he advocating something so namby-pamby?" It is interesting to me that the original Rough Rider understood the value of using intellect and tact over blood and guts. Sometimes people who have seen the mayhem and destruction are the very ones who say, "There must be a better way."

Expectations of Conduct in Collaborative Law

1. Participants will focus on the future and avoid unnecessary discussions of the past. Participants will focus on resolving conflict and not on assessing blame.

2. Participants will listen carefully to the goals that begin every four-way meeting, and will take actions and make decisions in furtherance of the shared goals.

3. Participants will address others in a courteous manner and tone. Participants will not interrupt when another person is speaking. Participants will avoid sarcastic, contemptuous, critical, defensive or judgmental communication/comments.

4. If a participant feels progress has ceased or that he or she is about to lose control and say or do something to impede progress, that participant will call for a break. If the break is insufficient to calm the affected participant, the meeting may be terminated.

5. Each participant will speak only for himself or herself. Participants will use "I" instead of "you" sentences.

6. Participants will express their true interests.

7. Participants will be patient with each other and their lawyers. All participants will assume that each participant is acting in good faith and realize that everyone does not move at the same pace. To pull together, each participant must sometimes accommodate by slowing down. Delays in the collaborative law process can happen with everyone acting in good faith.

8. Participants will follow the agenda for each four-way meeting. If there are other topics that a participant wants to address, he or she will ask that it be included in the agenda for the next four-way meeting.

9. Participants will be honest.

Provided courtesy of the Dallas Alliance of Collaborative Family Lawyers, 2003

3

A Brief Look at Texas Divorce Law

I t's often claimed that the first lawsuit ever filed in Texas was a divorce, more than a century-and-a-half ago. There were no specific laws governing divorce until the Texas Divorce Act of 1841, four years before Texas entered the Union. Most people who married either stayed married or just left the jurisdiction and declared themselves single again. Frontier Texas was such a big land that people could begin completely new lives in another area and the former spouse would never know about it.

Until the early 20th century, divorce was an option for Texans only in extreme circumstances, such as when a spouse abandoned the family, became mentally incapacitated or engaged in domestic violence.

Not until after World War II did divorces become commonplace. The number of divorces grew to almost 60 percent of marriages in the 1970s, and splitting up became easier and more accepted with the adoption of no-fault statutes.

Texas Family Code

As we say in our disclaimer at the beginning of this book, family law is not static, but changes constantly. Title 1 of the Texas Family Code was adopted by the State Legislature in 1969 and has been amended many times.

The code enumerates the various grounds for divorce in Texas, including:

• Physical and mental cruelty
• Adultery
• A felony conviction
• Abandonment
• Living apart for at least three years
• Confinement in a mental hospital

However, almost all divorces today are "no fault" and are granted on the grounds of incompatibility. The Code states: "The court may grant a divorce without regard to fault if the marriage has become insupportable because of discord or conflict of personalities that destroys the legitimate ends of the marital relationship and prevents any reasonable expectation of reconciliation."

If you have lived in the state for at least six months before filing your petition for dissolution of marriage, then you can divorce in Texas. Venue (the county where your case will be heard) is decided on the basis of where you have lived the 90 days before the filing of your petition. Although the law allows you to file your own divorce, couples with children or large assets should have the guidance of an experienced and knowledgeable attorney in navigating these difficult issues.

Child's Best Interest

There are several presumptions in Texas family law that pertain to children:

- ✔ It is in the best interest of a child for the parents to have joint custody.
- ✔ A parent is a better conservator than a non-parent.
- ✔ The standard possession order is the minimum possession of a child to which a non-custodial parent is entitled.
- ✔ If the non-custodial parent is unemployed, child support should be based on minimum wage.
- ✔ Application of child support guidelines is in the best interest of the child.
- ✔ The husband married to the wife at the time of the birth of a child is presumed to be the father of the child.

The courts consider many factors to determine the best interest of the child. Included among these are:

- ✔ Desires of the child
- ✔ Emotional and physical needs of the child now and in the future
- ✔ Emotional and physical danger to the child now and in the future
- ✔ Parental abilities of the individuals seeking custody
- ✔ Programs available to assist these individuals to promote the best interest of the child
- ✔ Plans for the child by these individuals or by the agency seeking custody

✔ Stability of the home or proposed placement
✔ Acts or omissions of the parent that may indicate the existing parent-child relationship is not a proper one
✔ Any excuse for the acts or omissions of the parent

There are some frequent misconceptions among laypersons on a couple of presumptions. Some assume that we have a "tender years" doctrine in Texas, meaning a presumption that a very young child needs the mother to be the custodial parent. In fact, we have a statutory prohibition against that notion. The court cannot consider marital status or gender of the party or child in determining questions of conservatorship, possession of or access to the child.

The other area of misconception is the splitting of siblings. Frequently, clients come into the office convinced there is a presumption against splitting siblings in a divorce. Actually, there is some conflict between the Courts of Appeals on this issue. The Texas Supreme Court has not spoken on this issue at this writing. The Fort Worth Court of Appeals has held that splitting of siblings requires "clear and compelling reasons." The Houston Court of Appeals has held that, although not favored, clear and convincing evidence is not required to split siblings.

Community Property State

All property owned by the parties on dissolution of a marriage is presumed to be community property. Community property is loosely defined as all property owned by the parties during marriage that was not owned by either party prior to marriage or was not acquired by gift, bequest or inheritance during the marriage.

Property owned prior to marriage or received during marriage by gift, bequest or inheritance is known as separate property. Clients sometimes believe that community property must be split equally, but that is untrue. There can be a disproportionate division of the community property estate, depending on a number of factors.

Janet P. Brumley

4

Texas Justice and Collaborative Law

In the state where aggressive "Rambo lawyering" has been an art form, collaborative law goes against the culture. The hallmark of collaborative law is that the parties and attorneys agree to leave their guns at the door.

"Many of the old-timers in family law sort of made up the rules as they went along," says Kevin Fuller, a family lawyer with the Dallas law firm of Koons, Fuller, Vanden Eykel & Robertson and a member of the Dallas Alliance of Collaborative Family Lawyers. "They figured you went into the courtroom acting as tough and mean as possible, and that's how you served your clients. To those family law pioneers, collaborative law is some kind of communist plot."

Texas is a state where every football game, business transaction, contract and lawsuit is handled with the most competitiveness possible. Working for the common good is alien to that mindset. Many people believe collaborative law got its start in the New Age, crunchy-granola atmosphere of California, but Texas was the first state to adopt a collaborative law statute, in 2001. This move may be the swinging of the pendulum away from a more predatory practice.

In collaborative law, everyone is working toward a final document that correctly and completely recites the agreement of the parties regarding all disputed issues. Neither attorney can allow a mistake by the other side to stand, even if such a mistake benefits his or her client. And neither party can utilize an attorney to hide or distort information. It's a brand new, but very old-fashioned idea — ethical legal representation of clients who want to honestly resolve their differences in a way that does the least harm possible to all.

"This is the way the law was always supposed to work," says Judge Robert T. Dry, Jr. of the 199th Judicial District Court in Texas. "Somewhere along the way, we developed this competitive environment for attorneys, and most people were looking for an edge. It became oxymoronic to be ethical and aggressively represent your client."

Communication between parties to a divorce under collaborative law and their attorneys is open and informal rather than restrictive and stilted. This represents a further swing of the pendulum, since Texas is the only state in which most family law matters may be decided by a jury trial. In the normally litigated divorce, the wife rarely speaks to or is spoken to by the husband's attorney (or vice versa) except when the wife is under oath and being cross-examined. Even then, the client is cautioned to answer as briefly as possible and always leaving oneself an "out."

This sort of communication is not conducive to the fair and equitable settlement of issues. And it probably isn't the best way to discover the children's best interest. In collaborative law, the parties and the attorneys sit down together in a series of joint sessions. In these joint sessions, everyone talks to everyone else about the issues and possible solutions. Sometimes real estate appraisers, psychologists or children come to the joint sessions to give their opinions on certain issues.

Unusual Attorney Agreement

A crucial tenet of collaborative law is that both attorneys agree to withdraw rather than go to litigation if no settlement can be reached. This solves the problem of clients claiming the lawyers fomented problems so the lawsuit would go to trial and the lawyers would make more money.

When a case is being handled collaboratively, it cannot go to trial, so no one can gain anything by pushing the case in that direction. Collaborative cases that fail can become litigated divorces, but the attorneys who could not bring the case to a conclusion have to withdraw.

It is obvious to me, a divorce attorney of 25 years, that even in bitter, usually litigated, divorce cases, husband and wife typically want to do the right thing. They just disagree on what the right thing might be. For instance, the wife truly believes the children need to stay with her on school nights because dad does not check homework, enforce bedtime or do the other "right things." Just as passionately, the husband believes the children need to stay with him on school nights because mom does not encourage the children to participate in extracurricular activities and she just wants to get them to bed and out of sight. To him, she is the one not doing the "right thing."

Using collaborative law, the attorneys might recommend that both parents take the children to a mutually respected psychologist. That psychologist could then recommend that the children spend every Monday and Tuesday evening with Dad (because those are the nights the children have dance and debate) and spend every Wednesday and Thursday evening with Mom (because those are the nights before their weekly tests and traditionally nights with more homework). Both parents recognize the rightness of the proposal. It's usually not that they don't value what the other brings to the table; it's that they don't even see it. You've heard that sometimes it's hard to see the forest for the trees. In collaborative law, the attorneys and experts are committed to helping the parties see the forest.

There are certain inviolate rules to collaborative law. We agree to turn off our cell phones in joint session, treat each other with respect and stop a session in mid-sentence if anyone feels out of control. Those of us who grew up in the South have another rule: always serve refreshments.

My mother would fry chicken for the electrician and make cookies and iced tea for the postman. It was simply an act of civility that, unfortunately, has been lost in today's fast-food world. I love putting out homemade guacamole dip or cookies and fresh fruit and, yes, I serve iced tea, as well. We all put on our best manners when we are breaking bread together.

Dallas Alliance of Collaborative Family Lawyers

I am a founding member of the Dallas Alliance of Collaborative Family Lawyers, the first group of collaborative attorneys established in the state of Texas. It was founded by a core group of highly-experienced, well-established family law attorneys, most of whom are board certified in family law by the Texas Board of Legal Specialization and have earned the highest rating by Martindale-Hubbell for knowledge of the law and ethics.

Twenty of the 22 Alliance members were selected by *Texas Monthly* and *Law and Politics* magazine in the 2003 listing of "Texas Super Lawyers." The point is that this is the first group of Texas family lawyers who have come together in an association for a very special purpose. This Alliance serves as a model for many other groups in the state that are turning to the practice of collaborative law.

The rule that attorneys have to withdraw and clients have to find new counsel if negotiations fail is a concern for clients considering collaborative law. Because of the Alliance, we can assure clients that if the process fails, we have a back-up system in place. The client can choose from many qualified attorneys who can take the case into the litigation arena. One of the first tenets of the Alliance is that any member agrees to accept a case from another member when collaborative law negotiations fail.

We also know that collaborative law requires two trustworthy attorneys. There are simply some attorneys you cannot trust to live up to the lofty goals of collaborative law negotiation. Members of the Alliance have to be lawyers whose word is impeccable. We also share with and learn from each other. We want our members to be experienced attorneys at basically the same place on the learning curve. We limit our membership to allow for good communication within the group.

Collaborative law is such a new and different concept in family law negotiation that we want our group to actively disseminate information about collaborative law to educate other attorneys as well as the community at large.

Since the formation of the Dallas Alliance of

Collaborative Family Lawyers, the number of attorneys practicing collaborative law in Texas has mushroomed. A comprehensive list of all the collaborative lawyers in the state is among the resources at the end of this book.

5

Mediation Without the Mediator

S ometimes collaborative law is referred to as mediation without the mediator. With two trained collaborative law attorneys involved in the process, it is actually mediation with *two* mediators.

Collaborative law attorneys receive training in many of the same procedures as mediators. While there is no collaborative law certification at this time, the best collaborative law attorneys undergo specialized training. Usually, that includes four days of education in the mediation process; two days of basic training in collaborative law; two days of intermediate training and an additional two days of advanced training; monthly sessions in a collaborative law practice group; and quarterly daylong seminars.

"Shifting the paradigm" and "reframing the issue" are techniques frequently employed by both mediators and collaborative law attorneys. Both of these techniques allow the party to see an issue from a different angle. You wouldn't expect a person without diplomatic education to negotiate a peace treaty as effectively as someone with extensive related training. A person with no education in mediation, collaborative law and interest-based negotiation is probably not going to be as effective negotiating a win/win divorce as an attorney with extensive training in these areas.

There is a definite learning curve for attorneys practicing collaborative law. Untrained attorneys are not aware that there is something they do not know. After further reading and training, practitioners require more of themselves in terms of preparation and education. They gain a real thirst for more knowledge on this subject and a need for self-improvement. The better the attorneys get, the better they want to become. It becomes a magnificent obsession once an attorney recognizes the good that can be accomplished with this new skill.

"The way I felt the first time I attended a collaborative training program was, 'Oh my gosh, this is what I've been waiting for my whole legal career,'" recalls Dallas attorney and former family court judge Paula Larsen. "It felt so right to me, to help people who have had a long history and connection to each other resolve these very difficult emotional disputes. Any other way doesn't make sense if you think about it. You take two people who loved each other enough to get married, and you throw them into a war zone when you choose litigation. The family courts do the best they can, but the system is not well designed to resolve family law cases. It's just not. But collaborative law is."

Houston attorney Donald Royall adds: "Collaborative law training allows the attorney to disable almost all the mechanisms learned in law school and expected in a successful law practice. Interpersonal skills that produce effective interactions between individuals are essential in collaborative law. We lawyers don't get much formal training along those lines, and this is probably our area of greatest learning need. These skills take training and practice to develop effectively. We must learn to listen for things other than what might be considered relevant and admissible in court, so that we can truly know our clients. It is essential that we understand and advocate our client's values and interests, not our own. Still, we are lawyers, not social workers or therapists. We need the training to recognize when those and other resources are needed."

Collaborative Law Attorneys Actually Listen

The attorneys in a collaborative law session are very active listeners who try to hear what the parties want, rather than just what they are saying. For example, one party might say: "I want to have the child living with me 50 percent of the time. I want to make sure he is properly socialized, but his mother just wants him to spend his life with his nose in a book."

An attorney untrained in collaborative law might focus only on the first sentence, thinking: "It's my job to do what my client requests. He has just stated that he wants his child 50 percent of the time. I will make sure, by counting days and even hours, that he gets 50 percent of the time."

An attorney trained in collaborative law will hear both sentences and realize the second sentence might contradict the first. The active listener will then say something like: "I hear you saying that your primary concern is to make sure your child is properly socialized. Your concern isn't that his mother won't make sure his academic needs are met, but rather that she might ignore his social needs. Is that right?"

At that point, the client will come back with: "Yes! He

loves to play baseball, but you can't expect him to play well if someone isn't practicing with him daily. I was that kid who made straight A's but never got to play sports, and I don't want that for my son. My dad was always too busy to play catch with me, but I won't be too busy for my son!" If the attorney had simply stopped with the 50 percent assertion, he would be off and running toward a goal that was never his client's primary concern.

Active listening helps everyone in the room understand what the speaker *meant*, not just what he or she said. Sometimes compliments are hidden in what first appears to be a criticism. Divorcing couples are good at never giving compliments to each other and not recognizing hidden compliments from the other party.

The trained collaborative law attorney can help people recognize these deficiencies. In the previous example, there was Dad's overt criticism of Mom on socialization skills for the child, but an implied compliment of her support of the child's academic progress. On first hearing, "His mother just wants him to spend his life with his nose in a book" sounds completely negative.

But a trained collaborative law attorney or mediator would reframe that issue back to the speaker as: "I hear you saying that you have no concerns that your child's mother will be supportive of his academic progress, is that correct?"

The speaker's response probably would be very positive: "Yes, his mother is great at reading with him and doing multiplication flash cards and things. She's always teaching him something."

If the attorney can overtly acknowledge the good in each spouse and help both parties hear compliments instead of just the criticism, he or she has helped repair terribly impaired communication lines. Instead of just teaching better ways to fight, the attorney is involved in a process of teaching better ways to progress beyond conflict.

You Get to Explain Yourself

The well-trained collaborative law attorney doesn't simply alter what you want or need, or ignore your concerns. He or she allows you to take the lead and explain yourself. For instance, the collaborative lawyer might reframe the example above and the speaker responds: "No, it's not his socialization that worries me most. It's that I need to have equal time with him. Socialization is just one reason."

Then the collaborative lawyer knows that equal time is the real issue and he or she needs to further clarify why equal time is important. The client might add, for example: "My wife and I have always felt that it was important for our son to have lots of time with both of us. I have changed just as many diapers, made just as many trips to the pediatrician, prepared just as many meals as my wife. My job hours are flexible and I want to continue this relationship with my son because I believe it is more important now than ever."

Now everyone understands what the speaker meant.

But calling collaborative law "mediation with two mediators" is not entirely correct. Clearly, a collaborative law attorney is representing his or her party and is not impartial. A mediator represents neither party and is impartial. A collaborative law attorney is expected to give legal advice to the client. A mediator does not give legal advice. These are the obvious differences.

One other difference between collaborative law and

mediation is equally profound, and that is that a mediator does not have to care whether an agreement is fundamentally fair or workable. In my experience, some mediators will boast that they don't care whether an agreement is good or terrible — they only want the *win* of a successfully mediated case.

This is not a successful collaborative law outcome. Collaborative law attorneys must help clients understand whether or not an agreement is substantially in keeping with prevailing law. Clients can decide to depart from prevailing law or guidelines in such areas as visitation and child support, but they will be making an informed decision. Further, collaborative law attorneys must draw on years of experience in the field of family law to determine whether a plan is workable. Once again, clients may overrule their attorneys' concerns, but at least the attorneys will have given the necessary advice.

Finally, a collaborative law case may employ a mediator if the clients' views are too divergent or their lawyers too partisan. Collaborative law simply uses a different path to settlement and may make traditional "Texas-style" caucus mediation unnecessary. Normally, in this type of mediation, the wife and her attorney are in one room, the husband and his attorney are in another room and the mediator shuttles back and forth between the rooms.

In collaborative law mediation, sometimes the attorneys don't even attend all of the mediation sessions. The mediator may suggest that the attorneys allow the parties to mediate on their own in the morning, and the attorneys come only for the afternoon session before any hard and fast agreements are made.

Problem Solving in Collaborative Law: Open All the Doors and Windows

One effective way to solve a problem in a collaborative process is to define the problem and the possible solutions and then examine the possible outcomes from each solution. I refer to this as "opening all the doors and windows."

Imagine that in defining a problem, you are constructing a room. Imagine that there is no way in or out of the room. You are stuck inside the problem. Think of each possible solution to the problem as a door or a window out of that room. No solution should be barred as too unusual for consideration. A possible solution that would have bizarre consequences might be considered, like climbing out of the chimney and then jumping from the roof. A better solution might be walking out the front door and down the steps. Both ways out of the problem bear consideration.

Once you define the problem (build the room) and list the possible solutions (install the windows, doors and other outlets from the room), open every door and window and look out at the possible ramifications of leaving by that route.

For instance, a divorcing couple has two children, one of whom is severely impaired and requires almost constant care. It's pretty easy to draw the room or define the problem. The problem is: "A father and mother have two children with very different needs. One of the children has special needs and requires almost constant care. While married, the father has worked long hours and earned a large income, allowing the mother to remain at home with both children. How do the two mature and well-meaning parents divorce and still meet the needs of both children?" Possible solutions to the problem might be as follows:

• Mother might continue to stay at home and care for both children while Father continues to work and provide Mother with income.

• The special-needs child might be enrolled in a day-school program where he receives both education and socialization. This frees up Mother to get a job and help pay the additional cost to the family for this program. The other child might be enrolled in an after-school daycare program.

• Father might exercise the flextime program available through his employer and keep the children part of the time, allowing Mother to get a part-time job.

• Father might stay at home and care for both of the children while Mother works and provides Father's income.

• The special-needs child might be placed in a live-in facility. The other child might be enrolled in an after-school daycare program so both parents could work.

• A grandmother or other relative might be engaged to watch both children while both parents work.

Once the parents list these options, they begin to "open all the doors and windows" and discuss the possible outcomes of each solution, as follows:

• Father provides income — Everyone knows the benefits and drawbacks of this arrangement, because it is the way they live now. The main problem here is if Father's income is not enough to float two households or if Father is emotionally or physically unable to continue being the sole wage earner.

• Special-needs daycare so Mother can work — This might be a great plan for the special-needs child, if such a program is available. Some considerations might be whether there is a waiting list for such a school, what the ramifications of this plan might be for the other child, the financial feasibility of this plan and the emotional ramifications for everyone as a result of this change.

• Father keeps children some of the time so Mother can work part-time — One of the real elements of this possible solution is purely financial. Can Mother make enough at a part-time job to equal what Father is losing in income by electing flextime? Also, is there an available job market for Mother's skills? Is Father trained to care for the special-needs child? Would the benefits the children might receive from more extensive time with Father outweigh the economic disadvantages?

• Father stays home and Mother works — This would probably be ruled out quickly, unless Mother is capable of earning more money or Father is more capable of caring for children than Mother is. The beauty of listing and discussing all possibilities is that often the party who makes such a flippant suggestion is the one who pulls it from consideration once everyone else addresses it seriously. For instance, with an executive who earns upward of $800,000 per year and a teacher who earns less than $45,000 per year, when we address this possible solution seriously in terms of how much money would then be available for housing, food, utilities, etc. to each party, the executive quickly realizes the ludicrousness of the suggestion.

• Special-needs child in a live-in facility and other child in daycare so both parents can work — One of the primary considerations here would be what effect this action would have on both the special-needs child and his sibling. Secondarily, there would be the considerations of availability and financial arrangements.

• Grandmother or other relative keeps children so both parents can work — Is there such a relative? What would be the costs and benefits of this solution?

The parties are now ready to exchange ideas on the possible solutions, armed with the considerations of the possible outcomes.

6

One Size Does *Not* Fit All

I f you are considering a collaborative law divorce, standardized approaches to problems probably are not your style. You're probably more mature and discerning than the average person. You don't want a divorce cut from the same cloth as everyone else's because you may have very different needs and circumstances.

One of the most surprising things to attorneys new to collaborative law is how many people in this process dismiss the state-mandated standard guidelines for child support and possession. As lawyers, we pull out our cookie-cutter forms and announce that standard child support for one child without special needs, of an obligated parent who "maxes out" on income (i.e., has a net monthly income of $6,000 or more) is $1,200 per month until the child is 18 years of age or graduates from an accredited secondary school, "whichever last occurs." Furthermore, "standard possession is every Thursday evening and first, third and fifth Fridays from the time school is released until the following Monday when school resumes, if school is in session, plus shared holidays as specified."

We are then shocked to hear the participants say that, with all due respect, they don't care what the Texas Legislature thinks is appropriate support or appropriate possession times for their child.

When you think about it, it is entirely reasonable to assume the two people who created this child, have lived with the child and shared dreams and aspirations for the child, are more likely to know what's best for him or her than does the Texas Legislature. But we have become so accustomed to the fact that this is what the court will order that we just agree, with a Pavlovian response.

"In the courtroom, we are constrained by the law; we have discretion, but it's discretion within certain boundaries," explains Collin County District Judge Mark Rusch. "In a collaborative law situation, you can do all kinds of things, come up with very creative and innovative solutions that work for one family but may not work for somebody else. These are the things I may not have the ability to do or the time to come up with in a litigated divorce, given the crush of the rest of my docket. With collaborative law, you can custom-tailor something that will work, and work well, for your particular needs. That's one of the best things about it."

In collaborative law, the parties want to custom-craft their divorce to fit their needs and desires. They do not want to be held to the arbitrary deadlines of the court, the attorneys or the Texas Rules of Civil Procedure. They want the privacy afforded only to parties who work outside the litigation system.

In short, they want the opposite of "one size fits all."

Who Favors Collaborative Law?

"Smarter people who are looking for a better way. Rational people, intelligent people, fairly well-educated people who recognize that the courtroom is about the worst place to resolve a dispute, especially when there are kids involved. People who are sufficiently mature to realize they can't live together, but they need to make rational decisions about property, debt division and the kids, and not turn it into a war. People who are truly interested in what's best for the kids — generally, these are the folks are who genuinely committed to staying involved in their children's lives. Those who want to fight and punish someone don't go the collaborative law route — they go to court."

—Collin County District Judge Mark Rusch

7

The Goodmans: A Collaborative Law Scenario

L evin and Kitty Goodman have been married for 13 years. They are the parents of a 10-year-old daughter, Anna. Kitty is not employed outside the home. Before Anna's birth, she worked at Texas Instruments and made approximately $50,000 per year. Levin is a dentist and makes $300,000 per year. Anna has attended the same prestigious private school since kindergarten. Levin is involved in an extramarital affair that he has successfully kept secret from Kitty. Kitty wants to remain married and doesn't know why they are getting a divorce. Levin is adamant about it. Their marriage counselor suggests that since divorce is imminent, they should consider collaborative law as their method of seeking a divorce.

Janet P. Brumley

The Initial Decision for Collaborative Law Divorce

To begin the process, Levin seeks out the names of divorce attorneys — family law specialists, as they are known in Texas — who practice collaborative law. Since Kitty does not want a divorce, Levin knows she will not get this ball rolling. He starts with an Internet search for "collaborative law" + Texas and gets the Web sites of a number of Texas law firms that practice collaborative law. He finds one near their home. The next day, he calls and schedules an appointment with Susan Martin, one of the attorneys he read about on the Web who is board certified in family law by the Texas Board of Legal Specialization and has many years of experience in the area of family law.

During his first appointment, Levin asks the attorney to explain the differences between a divorce using collaborative law and any other divorce. In the clearest and most client-friendly way possible, Susan explains the different methods for obtaining a divorce in Texas.

Litigation

Litigation is the form of divorce that clients have seen on television and in movies. One person files a petition for divorce and serves papers on the other. After extensive discovery and attempted mediation, the case proceeds to a trial by court or jury. Since Kitty and Levin have a minor child, their divorce will be known in Texas as a Suit Affecting Parent-Child Relationship (SAPCR). SAPCRs can be tried to a jury if either party asks for it. The court may appoint an attorney/guardian ad litem to represent the interests of the child if there are credible allegations that the child's interests cannot be effectively represented by either parent.

Mediation

Each person filing any cause of action in Texas must file an alternative dispute statement acknowledging that he or she will attempt to resolve differences prior to trial through mediation. Usually mediation is a one-day, shuttle-style event in Texas. The wife and her attorney are put in one room and the husband and his attorney are in another room. The mediator shuttles back and forth between the two for approximately eight to 12 hours, attempting to broker a settlement. The vast majority of divorce cases in Texas settle, and most settlements are reached during mediation.

Collaborative Law

Most collaborative law divorces consist of six two-hour sessions — the same 12-hour commitment required for mediation. The big difference is that the sessions are not all crammed into one stressful, pressure-filled day. Rather, they are spread out over approximately 60 days (a divorce petition must be on file in Texas for 60 days before it can be finalized). There are times when a mediator is used in collaborative law divorces.

Levin confirms that he is most interested in collaborative law. He discloses to his attorney that he is involved in an extramarital affair and this could intensify hostilities. Of course, he does not want the affair to become an issue in the divorce, if possible. From all indications, Kitty does not know about it. Susan explains that keeping the affair secret may be impossible. Just as Levin must tell the truth on interrogatories in a litigation case, he must do the same if he is asked a question during the collaborative law process.

Susan tells Levin his wife may be entitled to a larger

share of the community property estate if the affair is causing the breakup of the marriage. The affair can impact possession of his daughter, if the child has been exposed to it. Susan encourages Levin to discontinue the affair until he settles the divorce.

She also gives him brochures from several of the collaborative law practice groups in the area and asks him to share them with Kitty so she can find an attorney trained in collaborative law. Susan explains that collaborative law can only be used if both parties freely participate. Otherwise, the divorce must proceed in a traditional litigation mode. Litigation will entail interrogatories (written questions Levin must answer), requests for documents and all kinds of disclosure, depositions, hearings, mediation and a trial. Levin is eager to convince Kitty they can do this in an easier and less dramatic way.

Marriage Must End

Kitty still regrets that their marriage must end in divorce. It seems to her that Levin is happily embracing the notion of a new life without her, while she is still grieving for the loss of their old life. She never recognized that they were unhappy. Sure, she remembers Levin telling her that he was not happy, but he still laughed at movies and took her to her favorite restaurant on her birthday. Kitty thought it was just a passing phase.

Levin is ready to move on. For years, he has been miserable and has tried repeatedly to tell Kitty something must change. He is exhausted from his work and stressed from the pressures of financially supporting the household alone. But Kitty would proudly point to their lovely home and the fact that Anna could invite her friends from the private school over each afternoon, and she was doing so well in school. With each passing year, Levin felt more disconnected and lonely — until he met Kim, who sells dental supplies. Kim commiserated with his working schedule and seemed impressed with his abilities as a dentist. She complimented his appearance and noticed when he seemed depressed. Before he knew it, Levin's romantic heart, which had been in storage, was back in action. Levin feels guilty, but also exhilarated. The sadness, for him, is over.

Levin's lawyer recognizes a familiar pattern. Levin is miles ahead of Kitty in the process. And every good divorce lawyer knows a divorce travels at the pace of the slowest mover. There is no way to get Kitty on Levin's schedule. Levin will have to slow down and allow Kitty to absorb the facts, deal with the emotions, and only then move on to resolution of the issues.

Susan suggests to Levin that he not approach Kitty with a "Let's get this show on the road" approach. Rather, he should say: "I don't want an attorney to file for divorce and serve the papers on you. I really would prefer that we handle this in a collaborative manner. That way, we each hire a lawyer trained in collaborative law. Then the attorneys talk to each other and to both of us together and file the petition we want. They make sure it is not put on the litigation docket so we can handle this privately between ourselves.

"It is my understanding from speaking to a collaboratively trained lawyer that we have two years to settle this case collaboratively and no judge can make us do otherwise. Of course, if either one of us wants to litigate the case, we can. It's just that if the two of us want to handle it collaboratively, we can do that without court interference. I asked the lawyer I saw for a list of other attorneys in this area trained in collaborative law. Here are the names and numbers she gave me. Why don't you call one of them and let's schedule our first joint session? I think the important part is that with collaborative law, nothing is going to happen that we don't both want to happen. We can always decide later, if collaborative law doesn't work for us, to go the litigation route, but let's at least give collaborative law a try, for Anna's sake."

Below is the brochure and insert from the Dallas Alliance of Collaborative Family Law Attorneys that Susan gives Levin.

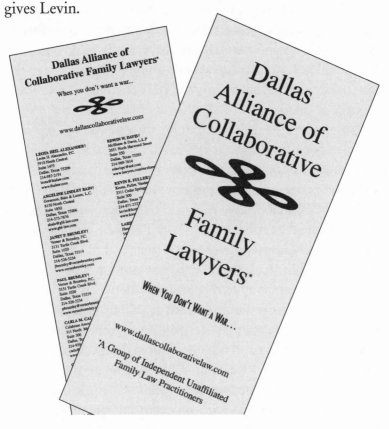

The First Joint Session

Levin calls Susan to tell her that Kitty has hired David Foster, and Susan calls David to schedule the Goodmans' first joint session. Since Susan's client is the more eager of the two, she agrees to draft an agenda for the first joint session (Appendix E). She and David discuss the pros and cons of reading the collaborative law participation agreement (Appendix C) aloud at the first session.

"Well, I know it's time-consuming for us to spend time reading the agreement aloud," says David, "but I have found that having each of us read a section aloud to the others is an action that bonds us all into the process. That way, no one later says, 'I didn't know we were supposed to do that,' because they had to read it."

"I completely agree," Susan replies. "On cases where I've agreed to skip the reading, we always have a problem down the road that I know we wouldn't have had if we had just read the agreement together."

Susan then goes to the e-mail program on her computer and sets up a new group called "Kitty and Levin C/L Group" and enters e-mail addresses for Kitty, Levin and David. She sends out a welcoming e-mail giving everyone her office address and telephone number and the date and time of the first joint session. She asks everyone to "reply to all" if they have any information to share before the first joint session. She attaches the agenda and copies of the collaborative law participation agreement, expectations of conduct (page 23) and the process anchors (Appendix F) to the e-mail, and welcomes any additions or corrections anyone wants to make.

Since the first joint session is taking place in the morning at her office, Susan orders sweet rolls from a nearby bakery, makes a pot of coffee and puts out assorted fruit. The most comfortable place for them to meet is the main conference room, but this room can be intimidating to nonlawyers. To make the situation less intimidating, she places flowers on the credenza and waits by the front door to personally greet the participants as they enter the office. She hopes this will lessen the tension, signaling a more hospitable and less formal response than letting the receptionist greet and place the participants while she (the busy lawyer) is on the phone returning clients' calls until the last minute before the session begins.

David tries to keep the greeting on a warm and personal level. As he enters the office, he warmly acknowledges Susan and introduces her to his client, Kitty. He mentions to Kitty that Susan's daughter attended the school that Anna attends, knowing that such a personal reference will humanize his opposing counsel.

When Levin enters, he is surprised by the levity and bonhomie he witnesses between his wife (who is showing a photograph of Anna to Susan), her attorney and his attorney! Susan greets him with a smile and introduces him to David. She points out that David's father was a dentist, and didn't he teach at the dental school, David? David replies that his dad had, indeed, taught at the dental school, but was now retired.

"Dr. Foster? Is that your dad? I had him my first year. He's quite a guy," Levin says, feeling much more at ease. This guy couldn't be too big a sleaze if his dad was Dr. Foster.

"Yes, and my brother is a periodontist in Colorado. I'm the black sheep in my medical family!" David laughs.

It is apparent to everyone that, although this might not be a totally pleasant experience, it isn't going to be the worst day they've ever had.

During the first joint session, the attorneys ask the parties to state the goals they hope to accomplish with collaborative law. Both parties agree their No. 1 goal is to minimize any negative impact on Anna's life. In addition, they want Anna to retain a close relationship with both parents, they want to remain friends for Anna's sake and they want to fairly divide their assets.

Kitty also wants to remain in the house with Anna and continue to not work outside the home, or to work only on a part-time basis. She and Levin decided 10 years ago that this was best for Anna, and she feels it would not be fair to Anna to change that plan just because Levin wants a divorce.

Levin does not agree with Anna's goals, but he keeps quiet about them because Susan had told him not to argue with Kitty in the first session, no matter what she says.

The parties agree that Susan will file a petition for divorce on behalf of Levin, David will file an answer on behalf of Kitty and both attorneys will sign the notice of collaborative procedures to be filed with the court.

At the next joint session, the attorneys will give both parties stamped copies of the originals filed with the court. The Goodmans agree to bring a first draft of their inventories after they receive a draft form and instructions.

Levin and Kitty decide to continue living in their home with their daughter and will discuss different living arrangements at the next joint session. They also agree to see a psychologist recommended by both attorneys for help in broaching the issue of divorce with Anna.

They schedule the next joint session in two weeks to allow the parties time to see the psychologist and prepare for the session. The attorneys advise that in their experience, the first meetings should be scheduled farther apart and the later sessions closer together. At first, there is a great deal of information to be gathered between sessions, and the emotions of the parties are usually raw. As the case progresses, there is less outstanding information to be gathered, and everyone becomes less emotional and more prepared to face the issues confronting them.

After the meeting, David sends a group e-mail summarizing their first joint session. He confirms the date, place and time of the next joint session and lists the responsibilities of each of the participants between now and then. Once again, each recipient is encouraged to respond with a "reply to all" for any corrections or additions to the minutes. This e-mail becomes the prototype for the agenda of the second joint session.

Most collaborative law attorneys like to meet with their clients privately at least once before each session, at a time of their choosing. Here the attorney can advise and encourage the client, who often feels uncertain and overwhelmed by the divorce and the legal process involved.

Some litigators do not like the handholding part of a divorce practice. My personal feeling is that if an attorney cannot comfort the client, it's difficult to be a good divorce practitioner. Our role, like that of the good physician, is part professional and part human.

Collaborative law does not lessen the client's need for human contact. It merely changes how we see that person. Divorce frequently brings out a person's dark side, the part that wants to obliterate the other spouse. In collaborative law, though, we see a higher-functioning person who wants to do the least harm possible to everyone. It is much less stressful to work with this high-functioning, rational person than with the irrational, hostile client. The other lovely thing about communication in a collaborative law divorce is that clients in that high-functioning state are better able to correctly hear what is being said. They are calmer and better able to process information.

In her meeting with Levin after the first joint session, Susan addresses two of Kitty's goals that might be problematic: staying in the house and not going back to work full-time. Levin tells Susan he has been a paycheck to Kitty for years and it seems that's how she wants to keep it. He says he doesn't make enough money to keep Kitty in the house, pay Anna's private-school tuition, pay all their expenses and have a life of his own.

Susan reassures him that no one expects this much of him. She doesn't even believe Kitty expects it. Susan explains that what Kitty really said was: "I don't want my life to change. I like it the way it is." Susan points out that she, Levin and David all know Kitty hates what is happening and this is not turning out to be the "money-back guarantee" marriage agreement she anticipated.

Susan encourages Levin to consider what he would say to Kitty about that issue in the next joint session. Levin says their goal is to affect Anna's life as little as possible, so they probably don't want her mother to starve or her father to go bankrupt.

Susan laughs and asks him to seriously address what he thinks Anna needs. Levin says they need to keep her in the same school. He understands Kitty would need child support besides school tuition, but he can't be responsible for much more than that over the long haul. Would Kitty need training to qualify her to reenter the workforce? Levin says he is sure she would, and he could give her financial assistance during that period.

Susan says it would be helpful for him to show Kitty that he heard her requests and took them seriously. He could prepare financial spreadsheets showing what it would take for Kitty to remain in the home, for Levin to maintain a home with room for Anna, for Anna to continue at the school and for Anna's college needs to be addressed — and how impossible it would be to do all that on Levin's income alone.

At Kitty's meeting with David, he explains that it will probably be impossible for her to remain unemployed. He suggests she look into what it would take for her to upgrade her training for employment. She doesn't want to work for Texas Instruments again, or for any corporation. She hated that job. It would be like starting over. David tells her she needs to consider what she wants to do, then, and what it would take for her to be qualified.

Bringing in Other Professional Expertise

Increasingly, your divorce attorney calls on other professionals — psychologists, real estate or business appraisers, accountants, investment advisors or divorce planners — to handle specific tasks outside family law.

For instance, you might have valid feelings of rejection, hurt, anger or guilt that need to be discussed and dealt with, and the best person to assist you in this would be a therapist. In collaborative law divorce, each spouse frequently has his or her own individual therapist, but they usually agree on one neutral and independent therapist for the children. This therapist may actually come to one or more of the joint sessions and give recommendations regarding the children — living arrangements, possession exchanges, overnight stays, right of first refusal and other details of the children's lives.

The neutral therapist can actually be a spokesperson for the children and their needs, and can help both parents understand the children's perspective. Parents often believe they know the children's wishes because they say the children have verbalized them — yet each parent has heard an almost opposite story. That's because most children tend to tell each parent what they think that parent wants to hear. When children are speaking to a neutral therapist, they can be much more honest and not fear hurting someone's feelings.

Children get put in the middle, between their two parents, so easily. "When one parent alienates the other parent with comments, suggestions or behaviors displayed toward the other, that is one of the worst things for the child," says psychotherapist Patrick Savage. "Think about it: If you ask a child, 'Who are you?' the obvious answer is, 'I'm 50 percent Dad and I'm 50 percent Mom. And if you say my Dad is a big SOB loser, that's part of who I am. And what if I love him? What if I don't see that in him at all?'"

Kids don't want to be in the middle. They don't deserve it, but even decent parents inflict damage and confusion on their innocent children. It's an extremely vulnerable area for many divorcing couples, and a professional therapist can help.

Neither party is obligated to accept the recommendation of a neutral therapist in collaborative law unless he or she has agreed to do so beforehand. A basic tenet of collaborative law is that nothing happens unless both parties want it to happen. Agreement of the parties is essential.

Appraisers are employed to value a residence or an interest in a business. The most difficult litigation cases sometimes involve dueling experts. In these instances, each side hires an expert who gives an appraisal most beneficial to the party paying the fee. If the husband intends to keep his business, then his appraisal will typically be low. A low appraisal means the husband must compensate the wife with a lesser amount of money. The wife's appraisal will typically be high, meaning she gets a windfall for allowing the husband to keep the business. The judge may disregard one or both of the appraisals or simply add them together and divide by two to get the average.

In collaborative law and less-contentious litigated divorces, duplication of effort and cost and the hard feelings resulting from the over-evaluated and under-evaluated appraisals are avoided by agreeing on one appraiser. This appraiser works for both parties, although neither party must accept even the valuation of an appraiser they chose.

Accountants can help value assets that carry different tax rates or have different cost bases. With their help, the assets of the parties are compared as apples to apples, rather than apples to oranges. For instance, $100,000 in a retirement account may not be the same as $100,000 in a residence or $100,000 in a rapid-growth stock, depending on several economic factors at the time of divorce. Also, the accountant can help identify assets that might generate income for the low-earning spouse and evaluate alimony as a deduction for the high-earning spouse.

Certified divorce planners (CDPs) are especially helpful to spouses who have not controlled the family finances during their marriage. CDPs can help these individuals generate feasible budgets and evaluate their needs. These experts work as a team with collaborative attorneys to help the parties adjust to divorce, which is as stressful and complicated as any divestiture of business interests, dissolution of a partnership or liquidation of a corporation. It is the single most important financial decision most people make in their lives, and available help is wisely utilized.

In a collaborative process, a certified divorce planner represents both parties. "The value of working with a planner is that it moves the process along more smoothly," says Maggie Tolbert, one of the first CDPs in Texas. "People who don't understand the impact of the decisions they're making tend to do nothing — they freeze. A planner can address their fears and show them the possible outcomes of their financial decisions. We help them identify their needs and explore their options for meeting those needs. We look at all aspects of their finances, including investments, tax implications and insurance issues. As the use of collaborative law grows, so will the use of certified divorce planners."

The Second Joint Session

The second session of the Goodman divorce takes place at the offices of attorney David Foster. He has sandwiches, chips and fruit on the conference room table and asks everyone what they would like to drink as he escorts them into the room.

Things are a little more stilted than they had been at the first joint session. Meeting with the psychologist and telling Anna of their intentions had been difficult. Both parties feel more at ease with the attorneys, but they are keenly aware that there is hard work ahead of them, and that work must be done in conjunction with a person who is hurting them. They both like the attorneys better than they like each other at the moment.

The parties reread their goals. The attorneys ask them if either one wants to change or comment on those goals. Levin pulls out paperwork and shows that it cost $52,200 to live in the house last year, including the mortgage, insurance, taxes, lawn and pool services, gas and electric bills. A comparable place for Levin would cost even more, if he didn't want to make a hefty down payment.

Anna's school costs, including tuition, fees, uniforms and extras, total $18,000 and will increase this year. Since Levin earns approximately $300,000, his federal income tax (filing as a single person) is approximately $100,000. He shows that when you subtract the costs of Anna's schooling, the cost of Kitty's staying in the house and his living expenses from the net income of $200,000, there is nothing left. He says their current house is probably too expensive even with them together, and it certainly is too expensive for Kitty to live in without him and all of his earnings.

Levin feels they must try to keep Anna in the school she has attended since preschool. He believes it was best for Anna to have an "at home" mother during her early years, but she is going to be in fifth grade. He feels it would not hurt for her mother to work outside the home.

Kitty says she does not want to move Anna to some apartment in the suburbs where she would be a latchkey child after school. Levin agrees that he does not want this, either. He points out that there are some nice smaller homes near the school, and Anna could come to his office each day after school and do her homework in his private office while he sees patients. Kitty could pick up Anna on her way home from Texas Instruments.

Kitty tells Levin and Susan she has no intention of returning to the job she held before Anna's birth. She has been thinking about teaching. That way she would be off when Anna is off, but she would still be working full-time, as Levin wishes. She has not had time, she says, to check into the requirements she would have to meet to be licensed as a teacher by the state, but she will try to do that before their next session.

David says it sounds as though both parties have amended their goals. He restates their new goals: to minimize any negative impact on Anna's life; to help Anna retain a close relationship with both of her parents; to remain friends for Anna's sake; to fairly divide their assets; to keep Anna in the same school; to make sure Kitty is able to live near the school; and for Kitty to teach. Both parties agree that these are their new goals.

The lawyers exchange copies of all the pleadings and give copies to the clients. The clients exchange rough-draft inventories of their assets and debts. David asks for a copy of the paperwork Levin referred to when he explained the available income, and Levin gives it to Susan for copying.

The parties address the issues they went over with the psychologist and agree that Levin needs to move out of the home as soon as possible. Levin agrees to move out the next week while Anna is still in school. The parties report that Anna is upset, but not nearly as surprised as they had expected. They agree to continue her counseling with the psychologist and make themselves available so they can address issues that Anna brings to him.

Levin does not want to upset Anna's last week in school, but he does want to discuss her living arrangements. He rarely works late on Mondays or Tuesdays and is off on Wednesdays, so he proposes that Anna spend every Monday and Tuesday night with him, and return to her mother's on Wednesday at 5 p.m.

Anna could stay with her mother Wednesday and Thursday nights and alternate weekends. Kitty says she doesn't know their summer schedule, but she asks Levin who would take care of Anna on Tuesday when she is with him. Levin says he has arranged for a woman to clean for him on Tuesdays, and she would watch Anna. Kitty asks if Levin thinks a maid should keep a child when that child's own mother is available? Levin says he thought the mother was going to be working.

Both attorneys recognize the warning signs of impending danger and interrupt with the advice that this issue could be addressed at the next meeting when everyone has had time to adequately discover and prepare alternatives. With that, Susan recites the agreements of the parties from that date, the next meeting time and place, and the responsibilities of each participant between now and then. She tells

David she will be responsible for sending out the group e-mail. Each attorney warmly bids goodbye to the others. The parties, momentarily diverted from their frustrations, reciprocate with farewells of their own.

At their meeting between the second and third joint sessions, Kitty tells David that Levin has never been the parent who took care of Anna. She says he didn't even want a child and probably doesn't even know Anna's pediatrician's name. He certainly doesn't know the names of his daughter's best friends, nor her archenemies. And what if she starts her period while she is with him? What amount of visitation does she have to give him? She certainly does not intend to give him a minute more than what's required.

David points out that one of their goals is for Anna to remain close to both of her parents. Kitty says she wants Anna to love her father — not live with him!

David explains that most studies indicate fathers who see their children more are more involved in their lives and pay their child support in a timelier manner. Most psychological studies show that children with two active, involved parents do better. He points out that you really need to be careful what you wish for with fathers: sometimes when a father is kept away from a child from a previous marriage, he simply remarries and has more children, effectively replacing that child in his affections. David says he does not believe Levin is like that, but he has seen it happen too many times not to warn Kitty of it. Finally, he reminds Kitty that she is a young woman, and Anna will go off to college someday. Kitty needs to cultivate a life for herself, and a couple of nights per week would allow her to do that. He asks Kitty to think about it and get back with him sometime before the next session.

When Susan and Levin meet, she says, "You kind of ambushed Kitty on that schedule for Anna, didn't you?" Levin explains that he felt pushed into it when Kitty insisted he move out. Susan tells Levin she understands, but you rarely get what you want with a surprise attack. She further points out that they might have to make some concessions to Kitty's fear that Levin doesn't really know what to do with Anna. That fear will persist until Kitty sees that his time with Anna is going well and Anna is happy with it. Susan asks Levin to find out what Anna wants to do this summer. Before the next joint session, he should determine how he intends to coordinate the summer schedules.

Kitty calls David and tells him she has heard from a friend that Levin has a girlfriend. Kitty asks if she and David could find out if that is true. David says that issue could be addressed in the next joint session if Kitty would like, but he doesn't think Kitty should bring it up to Levin outside the session. If David speaks to Susan about it beforehand, Susan will encourage Levin to reply truthfully. Does Kitty want David to call Susan about it? Yes, she does.

David calls Susan and says, "I don't know if your client is having an affair or not, but a friend of Kitty's called her and reported that he is. Kitty would like to address this in their next joint session."

"Does she simply want an acknowledgment that she is entitled to a disproportionate division of the community property estate, or does she want to directly address the issue of adultery?" Susan asks. "Because, I'll tell you, I don't think directly talking about adultery usually helps us move to an amicable agreement. It usually gets into mutual indictments of who's to blame for the affair."

"I don't think that's Kitty's intention," David says. "I

think she just wants to know if there's another woman."

"I'll tell Levin it's going to be a topic at the next joint session."

When Levin comes in with his schedules and sits down in Susan's office to prepare for the third session, she tells him of her discussion with David.

"It must have been Helena who told Kitty," says Levin. "I saw her one Thursday night when I was getting out of Kim's car. I was afraid she saw me. But we were just sitting behind my office in her car. And Kim is a sales rep, so that doesn't mean anything. They can't prove it's adultery."

"Look, Levin, in collaborative law, we all agree to tell the truth," Susan explains. "It is no different than it would be in litigation. You must tell the truth. You don't have to offer anything other than what you are directly asked, but you have to tell the truth if she asks you a direct question. I know you are afraid. You can call the session to a halt by saying, 'This session is over.' You can look down or out the window and just not answer the question, but you cannot lie. If you lie, I cannot continue to represent you. This won't hurt you that much, anyway. Just listen to her question and truthfully answer exactly what she asks you, OK?"

"OK," Levin mumbles. "I hope you know what we're doing."

8

Getting Past
the Need
to Get Even

The third joint session begins on time at Susan's office. Both parties look as if they are on their way to the guillotine. Everyone greets each other politely, but no one wants anything to eat.

"Susan, I believe my client has something she wants to ask Levin," David begins.

"May I say something first?" Levin asks. "Kitty, I will answer any question you ask me today completely truthfully. I do not want to hurt your feelings or tell you more than you want to know. I will answer exactly what you ask me, so please be careful to ask what you really want to know. And then, after today, let's put all this behind us and just move forward, OK?"

Everyone in the room looks at Kitty. You could hear a pin drop. After an interminable silence, Kitty asks: "Levin, why are we getting a divorce? Is it because you are in love with someone else?"

"No," he declares. "It is because we let our love die of

neglect. I worked all the time and totally lost interest in you and everything you did all day. I really didn't want to hear about committee reports or scrapbooks. You became a 24-hour-a-day mother and volunteer, and totally lost interest in me and everything I did. You really didn't want to hear about inlays and new epoxies. And then that disinterest grew until the only interest we shared was Anna. I still love you, Kitty, but I'm not *in* love with you anymore and I don't think you're in love with me, either. I think we're just both going through the motions."

"OK. That's all," says Kitty.

David prompts her. "He didn't actually answer whether he has a girlfriend or not, you know. Because you didn't ask him that. Do you want to ask him that?"

"No," Kitty responds.

"Thank you," says Levin.

"Let's take a quick bathroom break," Susan announces, noticing that Kitty looks close to tears, as does Levin. "Then let's come back and get to work."

The disaster is averted. Not by deceit, but by kindness, truth and basic decency. Levin agrees that Kitty is entitled to more than 50 percent of the community property without specifying a reason (Texas allows for disproportionate division for a number of reasons, including fault in the breakup of the marriage), and not another word is said about either party's character flaws. Levin and Kitty may not fully appreciate the gravity of the situation, but Susan and David realize they have just witnessed an act of grace.

Such moments are fairly common in collaborative law. Perhaps it's because just a small amount of truth, spoken directly, is enough for both parties. In litigation, truth is often hidden behind attorneys and lots of court paper.

Perhaps it's the atmosphere of the joint session that makes participants feel protected and better able to speak and hear. In litigation, there's a "gotcha" quality to anything you learn that would embarrass the other side. In collaborative law, there's a quality of maturity in the process. There is no encouragement to wreak havoc unless doing so will ultimately help you achieve your goals. The question the attorney frequently asks the client who is wanting to be spiteful in collaborative law is "Will that help you achieve your stated goals?"

That question has importance beyond collaborative law, to people who are not embroiled in a divorce. The collaborative law process forces us to ask how our current method of living is working for us. Are we conducting ourselves in a manner that helps us attain our goals, or are we working against ourselves?

In this scenario, perhaps Kitty doesn't think forcing Levin to admit an affair would help her achieve her goals. Maybe if she gives him a gracious "out" on this issue, he will extend her the same courtesy on another occasion. Maybe she recognizes that, ultimately, what Levin said was correct. Maybe she would rather believe that she and Levin destroyed their relationship themselves. Whatever the reason, an incendiary situation that would have blown up in almost any other venue is resolved with little harm.

When the participants return from the break, Susan asks Kitty if she has any more information regarding licensing as a teacher. Kitty tells of a program in which she could earn her license by teaching for one year in a public school at a lower rate of pay. After the year of teaching, she would be fully licensed to teach in the state of Texas. However, she also discovers that if she goes back to college for one semester of basic education classes and one semester of practice teaching, she could do her practice teaching at Anna's school and be more likely to get a job there for the next school year. Since she wants to teach elementary education, Kitty would be in a different building from Anna (who would be in middle school), but she would be on campus and they would share all the same holidays.

"Of course," Kitty adds, "private school will not pay as much as public school."

The idea sounds good to Levin. "But there is the intangible value to both of us that you would be on campus with Anna and off on all her holidays. It would be much safer and more pleasant for you to teach at a private school. How much is the difference in the pay between public school salary and private school salary?"

"It's only about $8,000 per year except for the first year, when I would be teaching at a reduced salary at public school," Kitty says. "But I would have to pay out money to go back to school and do the practice teaching at the private school."

Levin sees a solution. "Since I've already agreed to a disproportionate division of the community property estate, couldn't that extra money help Kitty finish her practice teaching? Could that be enough to pay for her schooling and still have her living expenses covered? I mean, if that's what you'd rather do."

"I would really like to do that," Kitty admits. "But what about the $8,000 per year for all the years after the first one? That's not a lot of money to someone who makes $300,000 a year, but it's a lot to a schoolteacher. Would you be willing to pay that in extra child support?"

"I've already said I would be generous in splitting

expenses with you over and above standard child support if you would let me have Anna for more than standard possession," Levin reminds her.

At this point, David and Susan interrupt with some suggestions on how the parties could accomplish what they want in a mutually beneficial way.

"Levin and Kitty," Susan offers, "the two of you could agree to split the assets 50/50 and make up the disproportionate division in cash paid out to Kitty over the next few years as alimony. Since Kitty will not be earning any income at all the first year and probably a pretty low salary the first few years she teaches, the inclusion of alimony as taxable income will have little, if any, detrimental effect on her, but the allowance of alimony as a deduction to Levin will mean he can pay more money to Kitty without decreasing his net."

David adds his thoughts: "And if Levin makes $300,000 per year and Kitty makes $30,000 per year, then you might consider splitting the expense of Kitty's taking the lower priced job 90/10. That is, Levin could agree to pay $7,200 per year or $600 per month, which would represent 90 percent of the shortfall on Kitty's income. That way Kitty is only realizing $800 per year less in income and is getting to work in a much safer environment and is more available to Anna."

"I would be willing to do both of those things, Kitty, if you'll agree to allow me to have more than standard possession time with Anna," Levin says. "I have a duplex with a bedroom for Anna. I've told Anna that I'll take her to pick out furniture and a bedspread for her room the next time she comes over. I want that to be a scheduled time she and I can depend on. During the summer, Anna wants to spend

Wednesdays with me, but she wants to spend the rest of the weekdays at home with her mother and friends."

"There are a number of ways increased possession time can be accomplished," says Susan, and she outlines several ways to increase Levin's visitation a day at a time.

"I could agree to that, but I could never do one week on and one week off or some other version of truly equal division of time because I think I have so much more time available to be with Anna than Levin does," Kitty replies.

The participants agree to consult with the psychologist regarding their proposals. They will continue this discussion at the next session when they can begin to nail down the details of settlement.

Tension was rampant in the room at the beginning of this session. But the participants handled themselves well and ended the session on a confident tone. They had not actually discussed specific numbers on the disproportionate division and difficult points lie ahead, but they are communicating their concerns in a mature and thoughtful way. No one exhibits any desire to hurt the other. On the contrary, both parties have gone out of their way to make life easier for the partner they are about to divorce.

Being kind has made everyone feel better about themselves and the human race in general. It is with some optimism that they tell each other goodbye.

"What is a reasonable amount for me to expect as a disproportionate division?" Kitty asks David at their post-session meeting.

"Actually, we asked our judges to compile statistics for us a few years ago on that issue," David answers. "It turns out that judges thought they awarded disproportionate division more frequently than they actually did. Also, they thought they awarded more disparate proportions than they actually did. In reality, it usually is only 55/45. However, in your case there are many reasons for disproportionate division. Levin has conceded fault in the breakup of the marriage. He has a higher education than you do. He has the expectation of much greater income in the future than you do. You would have more to gain economically from continuing the marriage than he. He has greater opportunities for investment than you do. You are going to have primary custody of Anna. I think it is not out of line for you to request a 65/35 split, but I think you should expect 60/40, best case."

"If our gross community property estate is worth about $1 million," Kitty asks, "then I should get $600,000 and Levin should get $400,000, right? And if we agree to split the assets equally, that would be $500,000 worth of assets to me and $500,000 worth of assets to Levin, right? And then Levin would pay me $100,000 in alimony the first few years after the divorce, is that correct?"

"That's right," David agrees. "And if you obtained 65/35, it would result in your being entitled to $150,000 in alimony. However, if you were willing to extend the payout time, he would probably be willing to pay that additional amount."

Meanwhile, at Susan's office, she and Levin discuss the valuation of Levin's dental practice. "Do I value the dental practice on this inventory and appraisement at the amount I would sell my practice to some other dentist?" Levin asks.

"No," Susan answers, "because if you were selling your practice to another dentist, you would also be signing a covenant not to compete with that dentist, and that would make the sales price for the practice substantially higher.

The courts in Texas have determined the way to value your business is what the business would be worth if you went into competition right across the street."

"Well, if I did that, the only value in my practice would be the inventory and equipment," says Levin.

"That's not exactly right. For instance, if your lease is for $19 per square foot and the going rate now is $23 per square foot, there is value in that lease. Also, if you have providers who send patients to you and would send them to whatever dentist was there, the profit from those contracts is part of the value," Susan explains.

"What do you think I'm looking at on disproportionate division?" Levin asks.

"Probably 55/45. I'd say 60/40, worst case," Susan replies. "It would be a good idea to run some numbers and possible settlement proposals before our next joint session, so we have some options to consider."

"Shall I value assets at face value or reduce their value by tax due?" asks Levin.

"Courts do not consider the tax ramifications of varying assets in division, " Susan says, "but we can in settlement negotiations. Just make sure that you do so across the board. Don't just reduce retirement accounts by the tax and penalty. Also reduce the equity in the house by closing costs and the value of your stock accounts by capital gains."

The Fourth Joint Session

The fourth session is scheduled from 10 a.m. until noon so the parties can extend through the lunch hour if they choose. They meet at David's office and settle down with pastries and coffee as each party pulls out spreadsheets and the attorneys exchange hard copies of rough, but much cleaner, drafts of the inventory and appraisement of the parties' assets. Susan has brought an electronic file of her draft for easy inclusion into the joint inventory and appraisement the parties anticipate signing.

First, the attorneys scan the Goodmans' comparative rough drafts for discrepancies in values. There is no need to discuss assets reflected at the same values on both Levin's and Kitty's drafts. The attorneys quickly ascertain that the parties have different values on almost everything, since Levin has utilized after-tax values and Kitty has utilized before-tax values. Also, it appears the parties have substantially different fair market values on the house.

"You can handle these differences a couple of ways," Susan explains to Kitty and Levin. "You can each do your own inventory and appraisement and not worry about the other's valuation until we begin to approach division of assets in settlement. That really just postpones the problem. Or you can agree to use either the before-tax valuations (larger numbers) or after-tax valuations (smaller numbers) and discuss your differences on specific assets."

"We should look at after-tax values because that's what the assets are worth," Levin asserts. "It feels better to see the larger values, but the larger values are not realistic."

"I don't know," says Kitty. "It seems crazy to deduct capital gains on stocks you have no intention of selling."

"Even if I don't sell them now, I will someday, and then I will have to pay capital gains," Levin says.

Kitty insists, "I understand subtracting closing costs on the sale of the house, but you're reducing the retirement accounts by penalties and taxes, yet you know you're not going to liquidate those, and neither am I."

"If it makes you uncomfortable, then let's use the before-tax values and I'll just keep the after-tax values in my head," Levin agrees.

"OK, well, even if you use the inventory and appraisement you compiled using before-tax values, Levin, we still have disagreements on the valuation of the house and the automobiles. Can you explain your values to us?" David asks.

"Yes. I got the values for the cars off Kelley Blue Book online and the house valuation is the tax appraisal amount," says Levin as he digs through his documentation to find the print-outs that support his values. He offers them to David.

"Oh, I think I see the problem on the cars," David notes. "The online version doesn't let you add in or subtract intangibles that are included in the hard copy N.A.D.A. books — such as mileage, special wheels and stereo options. Kitty, will you please give Susan the valuation documents we prepared?"

After the attorneys consult and ask questions of Levin and Kitty regarding their motor vehicles, they are able to come up with values on the cars that both parties can accept. However, the house valuation proves more elusive. The parties seem adamant about what the house is worth.

"We could either agree that we are going to sell the house and split the proceeds equally, in which case we have no need for an agreed value, or we could agree on an appraiser and accept his valuation of the property," says Susan. "I don't think David and I have any problem agreeing on Bill Russell, who is very good on residential appraisals."

David agrees. "I suggest we use Mr. Russell, since that will only cost us approximately $450 and we'll get a good idea of what to expect for the property. It seems like that would help us set an asking price. Also, he will tell us if there is something we can do inexpensively to positively affect the value of the house, such as painting the porch or replacing the back door."

The parties agree to complete the joint inventory and appraisement using "unknown" as the value of the residence, and to hire Bill Russell to do an appraisal of the property. David takes the marked-up rough drafts to his paralegal so she can produce a clean copy for both parties to sign before they leave his office.

It is finally time to proceed to real settlement talks. Susan asks Levin if he would like to discuss his first proposed division with Kitty. Levin explains that he has prepared three different scenarios for Kitty to consider.

Each scenario involves a 55/45 split.

"I believe that I am entitled to a much better disproportionate split than 55/45, Levin, so I am not interested in any of your proposals," Kitty counters. "At the very least, I think I should get 60/40, and I really think it's only fair for me to get 65 percent of the community estate."

"What! You want 65 percent of everything I've earned?" Levin exclaims.

"Before you get too excited, Levin, let's look at what 5 percent of the estate is," David interjects. "It is about $45,250."

"There is no way I can afford to make up that difference!" Levin maintains.

"But, Levin, we've agreed to let you pay it as alimony," Kitty says. "Why don't you call your accountant and have him calculate the after-tax value of 15 percent of our estate, or $135,750 paid as alimony."

"I think that's a great idea," says Susan. "Then we would have a much better idea of what we could all accept."

"And I'd be willing to spread that out over time so it would benefit you tax-wise," Kitty adds.

"Is everything going OK on the possession times with Anna?" asks Susan.

"Yes," says Levin. "The psychologist liked the schedule we suggested and thought it would work well for Anna. Also, Kitty admitted I was doing better with Anna on my overnights than she expected."

The attorneys reiterate what each participant is going to accomplish before the next joint session and leave together to call the appraiser.

9

Reaching Settlement on Major Issues

For the fifth joint session, the participants meet at Susan's office. The meeting begins at 3 p.m. so they can carry over into the evening, if necessary. Susan has put out protein bars and fruit, but asks her paralegal to come in and see if they want to order dinner if the session lasts past 5 p.m.

The attorneys have the house appraisal and enter its value on the newly prepared inventory and appraisement. Both parties sign off on it and the attorneys log on to the spreadsheets on their laptops to begin settlement negotiations in earnest.

The parties agree that neither of them can afford to keep the house and that it must be sold. They also agree that Kitty should remain in the house while it is listed and until it closes.

"I don't mind paying the house note until it sells, at least for a reasonable time, but do I get any credit back for those payments?" Levin inquires.

"Yes, usually you would be paid back at closing for any amount the payments reduced the mortgage. That would be paid back to you before the division of proceeds between you and Kitty takes place," says David.

"I think he should be reimbursed the tax and insurance portion of the payment, as well," Susan adds, "since those escrow amounts will be deducted from the mortgage pay-off amount."

"Is that OK with you, Kitty?" asks David.

"Yes, if Levin will make the house payment, I think he should be paid back at closing," Kitty replies.

As negotiations proceed, the parties agree to a 60/40 division of the assets. As discussed before, they divide the assets 50/50 and Levin pays the 10 percent difference to Kitty as alimony over a three-year period with the first payment due 31 days after the divorce is final.

The time-intensive portion of the division of assets comes in the personal property — cars, furniture, artwork, dishes and other household items. To expedite this process, the attorneys go down the list citing values the parties provide for each asset. Then the party with the greater value on the asset is awarded that asset at that value. On the assets where Levin and Kitty agree on the value, the attorneys ask which one wants it at that value. If they both want it at that value, they are encouraged to bid against each other for the item. Whoever bids the higher price gets the item at that value. If neither wants the item, it is relegated to the inventory for a garage sale that the parties agree to hold the next weekend. They will split the proceeds 60/40.

Finally, the attorneys have a division of assets that shows equal net values for Levin and Kitty. The attorneys then do a collaborative property settlement agreement.

"OK, now, everyone understands that this agreement is irrevocable, right?" asks Susan. "In the event this divorce suit ends up in court, the judge is going to enforce these terms."

Everyone agrees and all the participants sign it.

Susan and David go to the other end of the office and copy the collaborative property settlement agreement. The attorneys return to the conference room with a copy of the agreement for each of the parties.

"It's now 6:30," Susan says. "Do you want to continue and try to do a collaborative settlement agreement on the conservatorship issues regarding Anna, or would you rather tackle that another day?"

"I'd rather get it over with if we can," Levin responds.

"Me, too," agrees Kitty.

At that point, David produces a list of parental rights, powers and duties in the state of Texas and gives one copy each to Susan, Kitty and Levin.

David explains: "While you are married, you each have each of these rights, powers and duties, none to the exclusion of the other. That means that either of you can, for instance, give consent for underage marriage or enlistment in the armed services.

"After divorce, you can choose how to handle each of these individual rights and powers. For instance, take the issue of any non-emergency invasive medical procedures Anna might have between now and her 18th birthday. Or you can decide that Levin alone can consent to these procedures, since he is a doctor. Or you can give that power to Kitty. Or you can decide that Kitty and Levin each has the right to consent, subject to the consent of the other conservator. Or you can decide that both Kitty and Levin have the individual right to consent to non-emergency invasive procedures. Do you both understand the concept?"

The parties nod their understanding and the attorneys proceed down the list of rights and powers.

Parental Rights and Responsibilities

By statute, unless limited by court order for some valid reason, each parent at all times has the right:

- To receive information from the other parent concerning the health, education and welfare of the child.
- To confer with the other parent to the extent possible before making a decision concerning the health, education and welfare of the child.
- Of access to medical, dental, psychological and educational records of the child.
- To consult with a physician, dentist or psychologist of the child.
- To consult with school officials concerning the child's welfare and educational status, including school activities.
- To attend school activities.
- To be designated on the child's records as a person to be notified in case of an emergency
- To consent to medical, dental and surgical treatment during an emergency involving an immediate danger to the health and safety of the child.
- To manage the estate of the child to the extent the estate has been created by the parent or the parent's family.

Also by statute, unless limited by court order for some valid reason, each parent, during that parent's period of possession, has the right:

- To consent for the child to medical and dental care not involving an invasive procedure.
- To consent for the child to medical, dental and surgical treatment during an emergency involving immediate danger to the health and safety of the child.
- To direct the child's moral and religious training.

The difficult issues involve the right:

- To establish primary residence of the child
- To consent to medical, dental and surgical treatment involving an invasive procedure.
- To consent to psychiatric and psychological treatment.
- To represent the child in legal action and to make other decisions of substantial legal significance concerning the child.
- To consent to marriage and enlistment in the armed forces of the United States.
- To make decisions concerning education.
- To the services and earnings of the child.
- Except when a guardian of the child's estate or a guardian or attorney ad litem has been appointed, to act as an agent of the child in relation to the child's estate if the child's action is required.

Levin and Kitty agree that Kitty should establish Anna's primary residence within the city and contiguous counties, so long as Levin lives in the same general area. They agree that because of his medical training, Levin should have the right to consent to medical, dental and surgical treatment involving invasive procedures and consent to psychiatric and psychological treatment. Levin should make decisions concerning Anna's education, since he has agreed to pay for private school if given this control. They agree to share the remaining rights subject to certain stipulations.

Levin also agrees to pay for four years of educational and living expenses at a state university, or its equivalent value, if Anna is enrolled in a degree program full-time, keeping a cumulative grade point average of "B" or higher.

The attorneys draft a collaborative settlement agreement concerning conservatorship, child support and possession. After it is signed, they give copies to the parties.

It has been a full session and everyone is tired by the end of the day. However, they are also buoyed by the knowledge that most of the hard work is done — at least most of the Goodmans' hard work. The attorneys agree to meet before the next and final joint session to work out an acceptable agreed final decree of divorce. Kitty and Levin agree to be available to their attorneys by phone at that meeting.

The Sixth Joint Session

Since the attorneys have a draft of the final decree, the parties enter the conference room ready to sign the document. The attorneys allow them to read over the decree and ask any questions.The attorneys have also prepared the following closing documents:

- Power of attorney to transfer motor vehicle
- Operating trust agreement for jointly held property
- Letters to life insurance companies changing
  beneficiaries
- Letter to health insurance company regarding
  covered parties
- Letters to credit card companies removing
  authorized user

"Will someone please explain these closing documents to us?" Levin asks.

"Sure," David replies, "the power of attorney to transfer motor vehicle will allow Kitty to change the car title to the automobile she is getting in the divorce from your name to her name. The operating trust agreement for jointly held property delineates the agreements you and Kitty have made regarding the residence and how it is to be handled after the divorce — who pays the mortgage, who lives there, who handles repairs. The letters to the insurance companies are fairly self-explanatory. Of course, after the divorce, you and Kitty both want to change your beneficiary on your life insurance from the other to Anna, and these letters can do that. The letter to the health insurance company accompanies a copy of the decree of divorce so that your major medical carrier knows your only covered dependent after the date of the entry of the decree is Anna and no longer Kitty. The letters to credit card companies are signed by both of you to allow the credit card companies to remove the designated spouse as an authorized user."

"I have some questions about how we finalize the divorce," Kitty interjects. "I know we go to the courthouse tomorrow morning, but I don't know what happens."

"We meet at the courthouse at 8:15 a.m.," says Susan. "Once the judge takes the bench, usually between 8:30 and 9 o'clock, we go into the courtroom and wait for our case to be called. The judge will call us by cause number and also by style, which is 'In the Matter of the Marriage of Levin Goodman and Kitty Goodman and in the Interest of Anna Goodman, a Child.'

"Or the judge may simply say 'Goodman versus Goodman' or 'the Goodman matter.' We all rise and stand in front of the judge. The judge asks both of you to raise your right hands and be sworn. Once she has administered the oath, she allows the attorney for the petitioner to prove up the case.

"Since Levin is the petitioner in this divorce, I call him as a witness and ask him a number of questions to prove up the petition," Susan continues. "We will practice those questions in just a minute. Then I pass the witness to David for questioning. David may or may not have any questions of Levin, depending on what all I have already asked. Certainly, if David notices that some necessary question has been inadvertently omitted, he will ask it. Next, Kitty, I call you as a witness and pass you to David for questioning. Once again, David may or may not ask you any questions, depending on what I have asked you. At that point, I 'close' and 'rest,' meaning that I am finished with this prove-up. David closes and rests. The judge then grants your divorce according to the terms and conditions of the decree of divorce we have submitted.

"The judge hands me the file and the signed decree. You and Levin go out the same door you came in and wait for David and me in the hall. David and I go out a door behind the judge to her clerk's office and get copies of the decree with the judge's signature stamped on them. We then bring each of you a copy of the decree to take home with you. You need to keep this decree. However, you can always get more copies or certified copies of the decree from the courthouse, if you need to, at a later date.

"David, would you like to go over the standard questions with Levin and Kitty now?"

"Yes," David answers. "We usually ask the following questions:

> "On the date of the filing of this divorce action, had you been a domiciliary of Texas for the preceding six-month period and a resident of this county for the preceding 90-day period?"
> "Were you married on or about February 14, 1991?"
> "Did you cease to live together as husband and wife on or about the date of filing of this petition?"
> "Has the marriage become insupportable because of discord or conflict of personalities between the two of you that destroys the legitimate ends of the marriage relationship and prevents any reasonable expectation of reconciliation?"
> "Is Anna the only child born or adopted or expected of this marriage?"
> "And is she a 10-year-old female child born on January 1, 1992 in Dallas, Texas?"
> "Have you and your spouse entered into an agreement for the division of the estate and the conservatorship, possession and child support of Anna?"
> "Do you understand that you could have a trial on these matters?"

"And at that trial you may get more, less or substantially the same things you agree to?"

"And do you willingly waive your right to that trial?"

"Did you and your spouse enter into two separate collaborative settlement agreements signed by you and your attorneys?"

"And do you believe the agreed decree of divorce you and your spouse have signed and which we have this date proffered to the court correctly incorporates the terms of those collaborative settlement agreements?"

"To the extent that the agreed decree of divorce differs from the settlement agreements, do you want the court to rely on the agreed decree of divorce?"

"Do you believe the settlement you and your spouse made is fair, equitable and in the best interest of Anna?"

"Do you request the court to approve the agreement and accept and sign the agreed decree of divorce?"

"Do you pray the court to grant your divorce according to the terms and conditions of the agreed decree of divorce?"

With everything explained to them, Levin and Kitty sign off on the agreed final decree of divorce and the closing documents. They leave on friendly terms and agree to be at the courthouse the next morning to finalize the divorce.

It is too much to expect that this final session could be a happy one, but it is cooperative and the Goodmans part as co-workers and collaborators rather than as enemies. Even if the last thing they ever do together is peaceably dismantle their marriage, at least they have been able to do that in the most positive manner possible.

Reaching Settlement

Everyone knows Levin and Kitty are never going to be the close confidants they once were, but they are going to be friendly parents to their daughter, and every event for the rest of her life can be about Anna — not about Anna trying to make sure Mom and Dad are not fighting or glaring at or snubbing each other at her important occasions. If nothing more than that is gained, it is a huge victory.

Collaborative Law Process
Makes It All Work

People frequently ask, "Why must we have all these joint sessions? Why don't we just send them an offer or wait for theirs?" The answer is that the process is what works, not the intention.

Just knowing what to do doesn't make you do it. People know that eating less and moving more will make them lose weight, yet most are unable to lose weight on their own. They join a weight-loss program and they lose weight. People realize they need to quit drinking, yet they are unable to quit. They join an alcohol treatment program and they quit drinking. Why? Because the process works.

Collaborative law is not simply a process of chanting the phrase "Be nice." This is a process of negotiation. If you work the process, the negotiation will work. Simply hearing about the process solves nothing. Your friend may tell you about the weight-loss program, but hearing about it won't result in weight loss for you. To get results, you have to work the program.

Collaborative law involves interest-based negotiation. You must know what is in your own interest and that of your spouse before you can begin an interest-based negotiation. That is one reason honesty is so important in collaborative law. Everyone must believe what you say. If you tell us you want the blue car when you want the red car — but you think reverse psychology is the way to get what you want — you will be mistaken in collaborative law. Manipulating the system will only waste time and money, and may get you a settlement that is not what you really want.

Most people don't know what they really want when they begin. One person may simply want out. The other may want the divorce to go away. It is while working the process that they sort out what it is that they most want — not working while the children are still at home, keeping retirement intact or remaining in the home, for instance.

Participating in the program will help you become educated about your children, your assets and your debts, and that knowledge will help determine your goals.

Exchanging offers outside the process is almost always a bad idea. Here are two examples:

> Spouse No. 1 makes the best possible offer to Spouse No. 2. Because it came from Spouse No. 1, Spouse No. 2 doesn't like it. But, now and forever, it is locked in Spouse No. 2's mind as the floor of all negotiation.

> Spouse No. 1 makes a low-ball offer, knowing it will establish the floor for future offers. Spouse No. 2 is incensed that such an offer was sent. Spouse No. 2 is offended and will remember from this point forward that Spouse No. 1 wants to steal everything.

You can't win through shrewdness. They say they want an offer. In business, you give them an offer. In divorce, it will be your death. You can do it, but it won't work. Just work the program. It seems longer and harder, but it isn't. It's really shorter and easier.

10

A Different Outcome: The Goodmans Attempt Traditional Litigation

U*sing the fact situation in Chapter 7, here is how the same scenario might proceed in traditional litiga-tion. In this section, Kitty and Levin have never heard of collaborative law.*

The Initial Meeting

Levin visits an attorney the Monday after a particularly vexing weekend with Kitty. He has been unhappy for some time and thinks he is in love with Kim, a professional acquaintance with whom he is having an affair. He is certain Kitty knows nothing about it. This weekend, after all the discussions with Kitty about finances, she went out and ordered an $8,000 sofa. Levin could not believe it. He is furious with her. She never listens to his concerns at all. Her life is a cakewalk, as far as he can see. She just rides him like a beast of burden. He hates what a divorce is going to do to

Anna, but in the long run, he thinks she'll be happier, too. There certainly isn't much happiness in the family now.

Attorney Sharon Whitley has been recommended to Levin by a friend who has gone through a divorce and another friend who is an attorney, so he is feeling confident about his chances in a divorce.

When Levin arrives at the office for the initial meeting, he is shown into the conference room. Sharon comes in almost immediately after he is seated and introduces herself. He likes her carriage and her smile.

After discussing his situation for a few minutes, Sharon asks Levin what precipitated the appointment for divorce consultation. Levin tells her about the sofa and Kitty's spendthrift ways.

"Is she a signatory on all your accounts?" Sharon asks. Levin answers affirmatively and she explains that he might need a temporary restraining order to keep Kitty from wasting their assets during the divorce. Levin thinks this is a great idea. He has never been able to control Kitty's spending before, and after he files for divorce, she might really go crazy.

"Are financial disagreements the main problem in your marriage?" Sharon asks.

"Yes. She won't get a job and she won't stay within a budget," Levin replies.

"Who is the primary caretaker of the child?" asks Sharon.

"Well, Kitty is, because I work. She doesn't. So, of course, she's the one who's with Anna all the time. But I want to have Anna half the time now that we're divorcing. I'll get a cleaning lady ..."

"You mean a nanny," Sharon says pointedly.

"Yes, yes, a nanny. And she can clean and cook for us, too. But there's no reason Anna shouldn't spend half the time with me, since Kitty is going to have to get a job and she'll be gone from 9 to 5, too," Levin finishes.

"We'll need to have a hearing on the TRO (temporary restraining order) within 10 days of its issuance, anyway, so we can go ahead and have a temporary orders hearing at that time," says Sharon. "That will determine Anna's living arrangements, temporary support and such during the divorce. You know the purpose of temporary orders is to sustain the status quo. And the status quo in your marriage has been for Kitty to be a housewife and Anna's primary caretaker. To overcome that presumption, we would need to show some extenuating circumstances. Otherwise, I think you can expect to be named a temporary joint managing conservator and be given standard possession and ordered to pay standard child support plus temporary spousal support."

"What extenuating circumstance could get me half the time with Anna?" Levin asks.

"If leaving Anna with Kitty would constitute an endangerment of Anna, or if Anna wanted to live with you half the time and would tell a court-appointed attorney that, I think that would help your case," Sharon suggests.

"I think Anna would say she wants to live with her mother half the time and me half the time, if she were asked somewhere other than in front of her mother," Levin asserts. "She wouldn't want to hurt Kitty's feelings, but Anna and I are quite close. How do we get a court-appointed attorney for her?"

"We allege that the child will be inadequately represented by her parents and needs a representative appointed for her who will report back to the court with a recommendation," Sharon explains. "A representative appointed attorney ad litem must recommend whatever Anna says she wants. If the representative is appointed as a guardian ad litem, then the recommendation of the representative is whatever the representative thinks is best for Anna. Do you have any preference for which way the representative is appointed?"

"I think I'd rather that person be appointed as an attorney ad litem," Levin says.

"OK," Sharon concludes, "then I'll file an original petition for divorce, a motion for a temporary restraining order, and a motion for appointment of an attorney ad litem."

Kitty Gets Served

Kitty can hardly believe who is standing at her front door. After taking Anna to school, she is getting ready for a luncheon meeting to plan the school carnival when the doorbell rings. A man in a uniform is standing on the porch. When she opens the door, he asks, "Are you Kitty Goodman?"

"Yes, is everyone OK?" Kitty asks nervously.

"Yes, ma'am," says the constable. "I'm serving you with divorce papers and a temporary restraining order filed this day with the district clerk of the county. You need to read these papers and file an answer within the proscribed time period. You need to refrain from doing all the things listed in the temporary restraining order and you must appear at the courthouse at the time and on the date listed in the notice of hearing. If you wish to be represented by counsel, you need to hire an attorney before that date."

When he notices Kitty is crying, the constable adds, "There are times when I don't enjoy my job. You take care of yourself."

The room reels around Kitty as she shuts the front door and tries to read the original petition for divorce her husband has filed. She can't get past the heading "In the Matter of the Marriage of Levin Goodman and Kitty Goodman and In the Interest of Anna Goodman, a Child." It is viscerally painful to see their names in that context. There is nothing to do but cry. What next? Should she call Levin — that rat? He kissed her cheek goodbye that morning just like every other morning! Is he coming home tonight? What will she tell Anna? Kitty told Anna this morning that she would be back at lunchtime for the meeting. If Anna doesn't see her there, she'll worry. Kitty has to pull herself together and get up there with a happy face. She has no idea how she'll pull it off.

Somehow Kitty manages to smile and wave at Anna and her friends as they are going into lunch. Anna doesn't seem to notice anything is wrong, but waves cheerily in return. The other mothers are not so easily fooled. One of the mothers asks her what is wrong and Kitty breaks down. As she tearfully tells them about the process server and the divorce, she adds: "I didn't even know anything was wrong. I have no idea what's going on!"

One of the women says: "You need to get to a lawyer right away. My sister loved her attorney. He was so mean, he ripped my ex-brother-in-law to pieces! I'll get you his number." As she finishes the sentence, she is already dialing her sister on her cell phone.

"But I'm not sure I'm ready to see a lawyer, especially a really mean one ..." Kitty sputters weakly.

"You've got to get ready!" another mother insists.

"Kitty, can I speak to you privately for a moment?" asks Helena, the mother of one of Anna's classmates. She and Kitty are casual friends, but nothing more.

"Certainly," Kitty says as she walks outside with Helena.

"Oh, Kitty, I didn't know if I ought to say anything to you and I've kept quiet until now, but I think you need to know that I saw Levin getting out of a car behind his office late one Thursday night. When the car door opened, the light came on and I saw a young blonde in the car. I tried to act like I didn't see, but I memorized the license plate and wrote it down in my car. I've carried it around, wondering if I ought to say anything to you. I'm pretty sure they were kissing before he got out of the car. The windows were all fogged up."

"Oh, no! Did you recognize her?" asks Kitty, the lump in her throat returning.

"No, that's why I got the license number. I think you ought to go see that lawyer and maybe hire a detective who can check out this license number. Do you want me to get it?"

"Yes, please. I'm going back inside to get the lawyer's name and number," says Kitty, her resolve growing.

She gets the attorney's name and phone number as well as the blonde's license plate number. Now she knows what to do. Someone has to watch out for her and Anna, and it obviously isn't going to be Levin. She can't trust anything about him. She can't believe how lucky she is right now, though. As it turns out, the mean lawyer settled a case yesterday that was supposed to be in trial today, so he has an opening and can see her this afternoon.

Kitty Hires A Lawyer

Kitty waits in the offices of Mark Phillips and Steve Clark for about 10 minutes. During that time, she hears Mark's voice a number of times. He seems to be shouting at someone over the telephone. He isn't cursing, but he certainly sounds annoyed. And he sounds like someone who doesn't like being annoyed. She is fearful he is going to be angry with her.

But Mark Phillips is warm and protective in his manner, anything but abrupt or angry with Kitty. In fact, he makes her feel better just by being in the room. He looks like the kind of guy who carries a knife and knows how to use it. She needs a protector and this lawyer is an alpha male. His job is to sort this out. Her job is to stand behind him, where she won't get hit by stray bullets. Sounds good to her.

His retainer is astronomical, and she has no choice but to charge it to her credit card. She is relieved the card has such a high limit.

Mark (he insists that she call him by his first name) explains that Levin is going for split custody of Anna and has requested an ad litem, stating that Kitty could not or would not adequately represent Anna's interests. Kitty cannot believe it. Well, on second thought, maybe she can. If Levin is capable of kissing her goodbye on the same day he serves her with divorce papers, and if he has the nerve to slap her with a restraining order after kissing a blonde in the alley behind his office, she believes he would do just about anything. Clearly, she doesn't know him.

Mark explains that they need a psychologist and a detective, and lots of discovery. He says the general guideline for litigated divorce costs in Texas is approximately 10 percent of the gross estate. Kitty has no idea what their gross estate is. Mark says that is part of what they need to find out.

He calls Levin's lawyer and confirms that Levin will not be coming home to Kitty and Anna that evening. Mark also calls a detective and gives him information on Levin along with the license plate number Helena has provided.

Mark will file a cross-petition tomorrow, but they will not allege adultery. They'll wait until they have proof. Until then, Mark tells Kitty to keep mum about the blonde. He wants to catch Levin in a lie if he can.

"Adultery is valuable at the courthouse," Mark tells her, "but lying under oath is even more valuable."

Additionally, they'll ask for temporary support and set that for hearing on the date and at the time the other side has noted for the temporary injunction hearing. There will be no need for the temporary injunction hearing. Both sides will agree to a mutual temporary injunction, but Mark won't give Sharon Whitley a chance to agree to other temporary orders. He wants Levin under oath, and fast.

Kitty looks at her watch and jumps to her feet. "Oh, I have to go. Anna will be waiting for me to pick her up at school."

"OK, I'll call you as soon as I hear anything," says Mark, patting her back. "Take care. Everything's going to be fine. Levin is the one who ought to be afraid, not you!"

Kitty Tells Anna

As they walk into the house, Kitty turns to Anna. "Sweetheart, I hate to tell you this, but your father filed for divorce today. He's left us."

"What did you do to him?" Anna accuses.

"I didn't do anything to him! I didn't even know there was anything wrong! You saw him this morning. He kissed me goodbye and left for work. You and I left for school. Then I went to the exercise club, and when I came home to change for the luncheon, the doorbell rang and a constable served me with these," says Kitty, brandishing the sheaf of papers.

Anna runs to her mother, sobbing. Kitty wraps her arms around Anna and soothes: "It'll be alright, honey. I know you're shocked that he's left us. I was, too. But I'm going to take care of everything. You don't have to worry about a thing."

Anna goes to her bedroom, where she sees a card on her dresser. It has her name on it, in her dad's handwriting. When she tears it open, she reads: "Dearest Anna, I'm so sorry to hurt you. I love you so much. Everything will be OK. I promise. Hugs and kisses, Daddy." Anna can hardly wait to show it to her mom. Maybe it was just a bad fight. Daddy says everything is going to be OK.

Kitty is dumbfounded. When did he leave the card in Anna's room? And what is she supposed to say, now that Anna is holding out hope that this whole scare was for nothing?

"Sweetheart, I know you'd like to believe that Daddy is coming home and we're all three going to continue to be a family, but that's not going to happen. He's hired a lawyer and filed papers, and made it so I can't touch my money. I've hired a lawyer now, too. Daddy's lawyer told my lawyer that Daddy isn't coming home tonight."

"Where is he staying? Is he sleeping at his office?" Anna asks anxiously.

"No, he isn't sleeping at his office," Kitty replies, thinking to herself that he's probably sleeping with the blonde right now, while she is left to deal with an innocent 10-year-old with a broken but still trusting heart.

"He's not sleeping in his car, is he?"

"Of course not. He's probably in a hotel eating room-service cheeseburgers."

Anna whimpers all evening. Kitty wishes they had gone out to a movie or something, but neither one felt like doing anything. Everything hurts for both of them. As soon as Anna goes to bed, Kitty calls her sister. At least she can talk openly with *her.*

Kitty tells her sister the whole story, even about the blonde. First she checks the hallway to make sure Anna is not there. It feels so good to castigate Levin with someone who is inalterably on her side. She even tells her sister how Anna sided with her dad and how much that hurt.

What Kitty doesn't know is that Anna was in the bathroom when Kitty checked the hallway — but in the hallway while Kitty lambasted Levin. Anna heard it all. And she is crying herself to sleep.

The Temporary Orders Hearing

Levin and his attorney are busy preparing for the temporary orders hearing. The attorney ad litem is appointed and interviews Anna at school. Levin talks to the ad litem and she seems genuinely interested in Anna and their father/daughter relationship.

She even helps them schedule a dinner with Anna before the hearing. Anna seems unusually quiet, but happy to see her father. Levin feels hopeful about today's hearing. The only thing that worries him is that he has not told his attorney about Kim. He tried to, but she stopped him and said he should be careful to only tell her what she needed to know. He guesses she doesn't really need to know about Kim right now.

He saw Kitty when he went to pick up Anna for dinner and Kitty didn't say anything about Kim. And he knows Kitty. If she knew anything, she'd go ballistic! He wishes Kim could be with him this morning. She is such a help to him and he feels so much better when she is around.

Mark tells Kitty about his plan for Levin: "Listen, Kitty, I want to put Levin on the stand first. I want to catch him off guard when I ask him the adultery question. His attorney will object based on relevancy, but since they are trying to get court-ordered possession of Anna, I think the judge will overrule the objection and make Levin answer. Honestly, the fact that he has a girlfriend alone will not be of much benefit to us, other than on disproportionate division of assets based on fault, but if he lies under oath, that'll be great."

When Sharon Whitley sees the court reporter setting up for transcription of the temporary orders hearing, she knows to expect trouble. Mark Phillips is obviously expecting something this morning that he wants to preserve for posterity. Normally, temporary orders hearings are not transcribed. The court-reporting service is setting up a video transcription as well. In Sharon's experience, this means Mark expects Levin to lose his temper or lie on the stand, or maybe both. She instinctively leans over to Levin and whispers, "Let's go out in the hall and review my instructions."

Once in the hall, Sharon begins with her standard spiel one more time: "Whatever you do, do not lie or lose your temper in this courtroom. Don't worry about where questions are leading or what your answers ought to be, just tell the truth.

"Do not look at me for the answers, or the video will catch that," she adds. "Do not answer over my objections. Wait after every question and give me a chance to object. Then only answer if I have not objected or if the judge has overruled my objection. Otherwise, sit quietly. Make your answers as brief as possible. Give away as little as you can. Don't elaborate. Answer only the question asked, not what you think the lawyer is getting at. For instance, if he asks if you are wearing a watch, simply answer 'Yes,' not 'It's 10:15.' OK?" She doesn't get into a discussion of the fact that it is unusual that this hearing is being transcribed. The hearing is about to begin and she doesn't want to alarm Levin to the point that he will be unable to testify effectively. He already looks frightened enough.

As they return to the courtroom, the associate judge who will hear the case is taking the bench. The judge calls the case and the attorneys announce they are ready. Mark calls Levin to the stand. Levin knew Kitty's side would go first since this was their motion for temporary orders, but he didn't expect to be the first one to testify.

This is not what Sharon predicted when she went over the probable order of the hearing with Levin. She guessed Mark would first call Kitty, then Kitty's witnesses, and close with Levin. That way, he would have "tarred" Levin prior to Levin's testimony.

Levin looks with alarm at Sharon. She smiles confidently. There is no time to talk to her. Levin approaches the witness stand and is sworn.

"Mr. Goodman, we've never met before, have we?" asks Mark.

"No, and it's Dr. Goodman," Levin retorts.

"Yes, Dr. Goodman, I'm Mark Phillips and I'm the attorney representing Kitty Goodman today. Kitty is your wife, is she not?" Mark asks.

"Yes, she is," says Levin, loosening up a bit.

"And the two of you have a 10-year-old daughter named Anna, isn't that correct?"

"Yes."

"And you are wanting some court-ordered possession time with Anna, aren't you?"

"Yes, in the event that Kitty and I cannot agree otherwise." Levin is thinking this is not so bad, and he wants to look reasonable to the judge. He has forgotten his attorney's cautionary comments. So far, so good.

"Now, Kitty has traditionally been Anna's primary caretaker, hasn't she?"

"Well, since I work from early in the morning until late in the evening and she doesn't, she has been the one who usually takes care of Anna, although Anna's getting older now and doesn't require much caretaking by anyone," Levin points out. He is surprised that this guy is letting him get all this in. Levin thinks he is handling Mark very effectively. Why was he so afraid?

"Do you frequently have to work into the evenings?" Mark asks.

"Well, not frequently, but sometimes." Levin dodges that trap. He leaves it open, as Sharon and the videotape on being examined had suggested. This is an intellectual game. And Levin is smart. He's always been good at intellectual games.

"How many times were you at the office late this last week?"

"Let's see, I worked late on Tuesday and Thursday this past week."

"How about the week before that?"

"Oh, I think I worked late on Monday and Thursday of that week."

"Do you usually work late on Thursdays of each week?" Mark probes.

Levin does usually stay late on Thursdays, because that is the day Kim comes by his office. She tries to come late in the day so they can be alone after everyone else has gone home. Also, she comes on Thursday because that is the day the office manager is off. The office manager knows Kitty well, and Levin doesn't want her making some comment about Kim to Kitty. But this lawyer is just asking about Thursdays because Levin had mentioned working late on Thursday both weeks, or maybe Kitty has told him that Levin works late on Thursdays. That's probably it. The standard possession order gives fathers Thursday night with their kids and maybe they need to get on the record that Thursday is not a good night for him. OK, he is ready to answer and his delay has only lasted a moment. Sharon told him to think before he answers. This was probably why. "Yes, I do usually work late on Thursdays," Levin answers.

"Are you *working* on Thursday evenings when you stay at your office late, Dr. Goodman?"

"Of course!"

"You aren't out back steaming up the windows with a girl?" asks Mark.

As Mark predicted, this draws an objection. As the objection is made, Levin prays it will be sustained so he won't have to answer. The lawyer hasn't said Kim's name or even described her. He has merely used an expression. He is probably just trying to rattle Levin. But, true to Mark's prediction, the judge overrules the objection. "Dr. Goodman, please answer the question."

"I'm sorry. I don't remember it," Levin stalls. He looks at Sharon. She is looking down at her notebook. No help there. He looks at Kitty. She looks shocked, as if she can't believe her upstart lawyer just asked that question.

After the question is read back to him, Levin answers, "No sir, I am not." He waits for the roof to fall in or for the attorney to wave a photograph in his face or pronounce him a liar, the kind of thing you'd see in a movie. Nothing happens, and Mark continues with his questioning. Levin feels his heartbeat return to normal. Disaster averted.

The judge takes the case under advisement and tells the parties he will notify the attorneys by e-mail of his ruling.

"I think the judge really listened to me on the part about Kitty needing to go back to work, don't you?" Levin asks Sharon.

"Yes," she answers, "but remember, the purpose of temporary hearings is to continue the status quo."

The judge rules that Kitty and Levin are appointed temporary joint managing conservators of Anna, with Kitty having primary possession. Levin is ordered to pay $1,200 per month in child support and make the house payment as temporary spousal support. Kitty is given access to one of the couple's financial accounts for the payment of other interim expenses, but the judge makes it clear that any monies taken from those accounts will be subject to the scrutiny of the court as partial distribution of the assets. Levin is awarded standard possession of Anna on the first, third and fifth Fridays of each month from school's recess until the following Monday morning when school resumes, each Thursday from school's recess until the following Friday morning when school resumes and statutory holiday possession. Kitty has exclusive use and possession of the house and her car.

Fallout from the Temporary Orders

Kitty looks with dismay at the faxed copy of the master's recommendation that she receives from her attorney. Levin has only been ordered to pay the house payment as spousal support, plus $1,200 per month as child support. The mortgage accounts for only $3,000 of the normal $4,350 per month the couple spends on household upkeep. It doesn't cover the utilities, the lawn service or the pool service. It also doesn't cover the maid. And Kitty testified that Anna's normal school expenses alone are approximately $1,500 per month.

"What am I supposed to do about money?" Kitty asks Mark when she finally reaches him by telephone later that day. "There's not enough child support ordered to even cover Anna's school costs, and the spousal support Levin was ordered to pay is only the monthly mortgage."

"Well, you were given permission to invade the savings account, although I think you'd better restrict that to payment of litigation expenses, like attorneys' fees and court reporters and experts," Mark replies. "We can appeal the ruling, or you can get a job to supplement your income."

"But Anna really needs me right now. She is unusually clingy and stays right by my side after I pick her up each day from school. What about an appeal?"

"I have to tell you, the court usually does not reverse or amend the rulings of its master, unless there is some real travesty. Why don't you see if you can get your old job back at Texas Instruments?" Mark suggests.

"I don't really want to go back to the business world," Kitty replies.

"I understand, but you also don't want to be perceived by the court as being unwilling to work, especially since you are in a court with a judge whose wife has always been a working mother and whose court reporter is a working mother," Mark counters. "Besides, the best part of the temporary orders hearing is that Levin lied on the stand. And we're going to be able to show it. Right now, we need to hire a detective to track down the owner of that car Levin was in."

All in all, Levin is pleased with the master's recommendation. The monetary rulings are acceptable, although he wishes the judge had restricted Kitty's access to the financial account. Most important, however, it appears that Kitty's lawyer was just fishing on the "steaming up the car windows" comment.

Levin tells Kim they have to stay away from one another during the divorce. She cries and they both realize they can't stay away from each other until it's over. They'll just have to be smart. Kim won't come to his apartment or he to hers. Clearly, they can't make out in her car anymore. They decide they will meet at a hotel next to a mall. Then it will look like Levin is going shopping. He'll have Kim rent the room — he certainly can't put it on his credit card. Then, after he browses store windows and is sure no one is following him, he'll go to the room where Kim waits. They will come and go separately. And he'll make sure he leaves before the last store or restaurant closes, so he has an excuse for being there, just in case he is noticed.

One thing Levin can't understand is that right after the fax of the master's recommendation, he receives a long list of questions from Kitty's lawyer that Levin must answer under oath. Also, there are pages of documents Mark Phillips wants and Sharon Whitley says Levin will have to produce in the next 30 days. Levin looks over the questions and many of them are similar to the questions asked in the hearing. Sharon explains that all the questions — which she calls interrogatories — are standard and simply need to be truthfully answered.

The only one that makes Levin nervous deals with adultery. He rationalizes that what he and Kim share is not an adulterous affair. He is in love with her and is getting a divorce to be with her. She isn't some tawdry one-night stand. And he knows, for Kim's and Anna's sake, he will never admit to having had sex with Kim. It isn't gentlemanly, and he is a gentleman. He thinks Mark Phillips is a cad for asking the question.

The Detective's Report

It doesn't take the detective long to run the license plate and discover that the owner of the vehicle is a Kim Walker. From there, he discovers that Kim sells dental equipment, is 5-foot-6, weighs 113 pounds, is 26 years of age, lives in an apartment in Dallas and has never been married.

Upon hearing these facts, Mark decides to wait until Levin gives his responses to discovery. Regardless of what Mark said to Kitty earlier, they don't actually have Levin denying adultery. They do have him denying the specific testimony of Kitty's friend, but Mark wants more. He knows that if there are no more waves, Levin is likely to deny adultery in writing, under oath. And each lie makes the next lie easier. Then he'll get Levin to deny it again in his deposition. Only after he documents the lie three times will Mark start deposing Levin's office staff as well as Kim Walker and her roommates. He bets anything Kim has told somebody. And he hopes Levin loves this girl and wants to protect her. Then he can really get a good settlement for Kitty. He just hopes Levin doesn't get word that they are on to him.

Mark tells the detective to follow Kim. He wants to know her friends, her roommates, where she hangs out and with whom. Most of all, he wants photos of her with Levin. He figures Levin has told her he can't see her, but suspects he'll slip up. Mark just hopes he slips up while the detective is watching.

Mark and Kitty get lucky. The day the detective begins to follow Kim, she goes to Levin's office, ostensibly on a sales call. At the end of the sales call, Levin walks Kim to her car. It is beginning to get dark, but the detective has no problem getting pictures of Kim brushing Levin's wind-blown hair back and Levin touching Kim's face with his fingertips as she gets in her car. There are no kisses. There is no handholding. But there is no mistaking the yearning.

The detective thinks they are finished for the day, but later Kim goes to a high-rise hotel. It is attached to a mall, and he theorizes that she might have simply parked by the hotel, planning to go into the mall. He gets out of the car and follows her in. She is at the check-in desk. In a few minutes, she goes to the elevators. The detective gets photographs of her at both places. Then he settles into a comfortable chair and reads while he waits for Levin to appear.

When Levin shows up, the detective takes photos of him entering from the mall and getting on the elevator. Then the detective calls his agency and asks a female counterpart to relieve him. He wants photos of Kim and Levin leaving the hotel, but he knows one or both may notice the man who passed them as they entered also passed them as they exited.

The female detective has a large hairdo and wears brightly colored Escada clothing. She has learned the best way to blend in is to look flamboyant. No one suspects that a flamboyantly dressed person is trying not to be noticed. She views the digital photos taken by the male detective earlier that evening and knows the parties will be wearing the same clothing. However, she suspects Levin might take the stairs so she locates the emergency stairways. The concierge assumes she is a guest and explains that the stairs are on each end of the floors. He shows her where they open onto the lobby. The doors to the stairway are heavy and would be conspicuous if opened, but it is difficult to watch both of them and the elevator bank simultaneously. The female detective decides to bring in another detective to watch the doors to the stairs while she takes the elevator bank. As it turns out, Levin exits through a stairway and the detective captures excellent photos. The digital time shows that Levin has spent two hours and seven minutes in the hotel. The detective follows him through the mall as Levin conspicuously enters a Williams-Sonoma store and makes a purchase of jelly before exiting from a mall entrance to his car, which is parked on the opposite side of the mall from the hotel and Kim's car. He is whistling and swinging the bag. The detective gets a shot of that, as well.

Meanwhile, the female detective not only gets photos of Kim — she literally runs into her and apologizes profusely, explaining that she is on her way to meet her boyfriend and wasn't watching where she was going. Kim laughs and says that she completely understands. The female detective confides that Kim looks like she is in love. Kim says, "I am!" and walks on.

The Wind-Up

When Mark gets the responses from Levin and sees the denials, he whoops with delight. They have him! Moving in for the kill, the attorney attempts to schedule depositions. Sharon won't schedule any depositions until she receives the responses to her discovery, however. Mark backs off, knowing this is as good as it's going to get.

When Sharon sees the detective's report in Kitty's responses to discovery, she calls Mark and suggests they schedule a mediation date before the parties incur any more attorneys' fees by doing depositions. At mediation, they settle the case with a disproportionate division of the estate due to fault in the breakup of the marriage and other factors. Approximately $150,000 of the estate has been depleted in attorneys' fees and other costs of litigation, leaving a community estate of $850,000. Levin agrees to take his practice, valued at $300,000, and his car, valued at $40,000, as his sole and separate property. Kitty takes the house — which will have to be sold — plus the furnishings, her car and the retirement accounts. The mutual fund accounts and Anna's college fund are gone.

Kitty will not agree to joint managing conservatorship. Since Anna has learned about Kim, she hates her father and does not even want to see him during standard possession times. Kitty trades away Levin's offer to pay for Anna's private school and college (if he could have equal time with Anna) for making Anna happy. The final agreement is that Levin will pay standard child support only and will see Anna only when the girl wants to see him.

Levin despises Kitty more than he ever thought possible. The saying "There is no fury like that of a woman scorned" is really true! She has killed his relationship with Anna out of pure vindictiveness. She has told everyone that he is a lying cheat! On her responses to discovery, the list of people with knowledge is unbelievable. It includes everyone they'd ever *thought* about knowing. The upside is that there is no need to keep Kim a secret anymore. Everyone already knows, anyway — Kitty has made sure of that. It doesn't help that Kim says Anna is probably going to be just like her mother. It hurts Kim to see how much Anna has hurt Levin. She doesn't care if they never see Anna again. She tells Levin he has been a great father and she can't believe how Anna has rejected him. They will just have a family of their own. Her children would never treat Levin the way Anna has, just as she would never become Kitty. Or, at least, that's what she thinks.

Kitty is crushed. Her whole life has been a lie. Levin was never the knight in shining armor who loved her and Anna. He was just a lying cheat. And he is selfish. He doesn't care if she and Anna have to do without. He doesn't even care if Anna doesn't get to finish at the school they chose for her years ago. All he cares about is using his money as control. Well, she showed him!

Anna is a changed child. Her father has left. They have to sell their house. Her mother works long hours and is not the smiling mom she's always known. Anna will go to a new school next year. And, worst of all, her father's girlfriend is always with him. She has asked her mom and her lawyer to make sure she doesn't have to go over there. But secretly she hopes her dad will say, "I cannot and will not do without Anna! Whatever I must do to see her, I will do!" That's how parents are supposed to feel, right? It doesn't happen. She figures she just isn't worth much to him.

11

Collaborative Law and the Unequal Couple

Cedric Allen and his wife, Martha, have been married for 27 years. Cedric owns a successful business. Martha, by mutual agreement, has stayed home and reared the children, who are now grown. Cedric has always decided where they live, what clubs they join, where and when they vacation and which financial investments they make. Martha has always just gone along with what he wanted. Cedric has to manage more and more as his company grows, and he is accustomed to a very fast pace. Martha has less to do and more time to do it, and is accustomed to a slow-paced lifestyle. Cedric makes decisions quickly and moves on. Martha agonizes over decisions. Cedric is very athletic and in good shape for his age (57); Martha (52) gardens, has had a

10 Keys to a Collaborative Law Divorce

1. Identify your goals.
Recognize that your life is separate from your spouse's. You cannot micromanage your spouse's life. With divorce you lose this control, if it was ever yours to begin with. This means that you cannot dictate that your spouse get a job, quit being a workaholic, etc. Your goals need to be important and general, rather than small and specific, e.g., securing your children's continued parental support in their endeavors rather than "I want their father to pay for college."

2. Look forward to achieving your goals rather than backward in the blame game.
Don't confuse hurting your spouse with progress. Gratuitous harm is never helpful to anyone. It always bites you. This means do not gossip, criticize or be sarcastic, flippant or hurtful, or in any other way self-destructive. None of these behaviors will help you achieve your goals. Behaving in a courteous and professional way will.

3. Participate constructively in the scheduled joint sessions.
Remember, nothing can happen unless you agree to it. So relax and consider all the possibilities. It cannot hurt you to politely hear and consider your soon-to-be ex's ideas.

4. Heed advice from experts.
Leave your mind open to the possibility that your Aunt Heidi and your father may be wrong about some things — including the terms of your divorce.

5. Be truthful in the kindest way possible.

In interest-based negotiation, everyone needs to know what you need. Tell them.

6. Be patient.

You may have gotten married less than two months after your proposal, but you won't get divorced as quickly as you think you should. Your spouse has a timetable, too, and it may not be the same as yours.

7. Be helpful.

Realize that helping your spouse get the information that he or she needs helps you to attain what is surely one of your goals — to learn to work with your spouse in a cooperative spirit.

8. Think outside the box.

Break down your divorce to specific problems, e.g., "How will I live financially?" With each problem, define the problem ("build the room"); name all possible solutions, no matter how absurd ("put in the windows and doors"); examine the consequences of each solution ("open each door and window and look outside"); then determine the best solution ("identify the front door").

9. Expect some conflict.

Remember, this is conflict resolution, not conflict-free resolution.

10. Negotiate constructively.

Don't just disregard offers. Listen to what your spouse says that he or she needs and attempt to accommodate those needs.

malignancy removed from her face and now must watch her time in the sun. She suffers from depression. Cedric is the one wanting the divorce. He feels guilty about it, but he does not want to spend his retirement years with this woman with whom he has little in common, other than their children. He visits a lawyer recommended to him by his corporate attorney. The divorce attorney, Debra Livingston, explains collaborative law to Cedric and he feels it would be beneficial for him and Martha. After Cedric speaks to Martha about collaborative law and gives her the list of attorneys who practice in their area, she asks their son to interview the attorneys with her. The following is a birds-eye view of one of those interviews, with an attorney named Paula Clayton.

"Good morning, I'm Paula," the attorney says as she enters the conference room where Martha Allen and her son are waiting.

"I'm Jeff Allen and this is my mother, Martha Allen," says the son, who fills in as many details of his parents' lives as possible. "My mother and father have been married for many years and my father has decided he wants a divorce. My dad is a very strong man who is very much in control. My mom has never really known anything about their finances. Now my dad is recommending collaborative law as a way to handle this divorce. We like the way it sounds, all friendly and everything, but my sister and I are concerned that my mother be adequately protected. And we're just afraid this is another way for Dad to be in control of Mom."

Noting that the son is speaking for his mother and taking over the initial interview, Paula Clayton gets her first glimpse of her client's passivity. Most divorce lawyers recognize that passivity can be a sword as well as a shield, and Paula sees that Martha's passivity has already resulted in both of her children being enlisted as her protectors.

The Hidden Asset Problem

"Are you worried about your husband controlling the process, Mrs. Allen?" Paula asks.

"I guess what I'm worried about most is Cedric hiding our money," Martha replies. "I don't know what we own. He's always given me money to run the house, and he's handled everything else. In the last few years, I haven't even felt like handling the bills at the house, so Cedric took those over, too. Remember, Jeff, after the first time I went into the hospital, how Dad got so mad because our checking account was overdrawn and the bank manager told him he usually let me 'float' a day or two until Dad gave me my next allowance for deposit? Anyway, I'm sorry, I'm off the subject again. I have depression problems and it's hard for me to concentrate when I'm on the medication."

"There are ways to address your concerns and Jeff's with collaborative law," the attorney explains. "First of all, we will require that Cedric prepare a sworn inventory and appraisement, listing all of your assets and liabilities. Literally, it will list every bank account, mutual fund, retirement account, motor vehicle, trust, artwork, furnishing and household item. Then we will provide for the decree to order that any asset held by either of you that is not disclosed in the inventory and appraisement be awarded to the person not in possession. That way, if you ever find there is some asset which Cedric did not disclose, you can claim it."

"Still, we'd have to find out that the asset exists, right? What if we never know it exists?" asks Jeff.

"That is the same problem you would have with a normally litigated divorce. You must prove an asset exists before it can be awarded to you. That is no different in collaborative law than in litigation," Paula notes. "And to address your earlier concern, Jeff, that your father will use the process of collaborative law to control your mother through the divorce, I want to explain a few things.

"First of all, a joint session — that is, a session with both parties and their lawyers — can be stopped dead in its tracks with the statement "This session is over" by any one of the four participants if that is negotiated at the first session. We will suggest at the first session that any time any one of the participants feels overwhelmed, threatened, angry, overly upset or fearful that continuing the session will result in losing headway, he or she may end the session and all the other participants will quietly gather their things and leave without so much as a goodbye being spoken. This is done to ensure that none of the participants uses manipulative or controlling tactics to bully their way to an agreement that will be rescinded at the next meeting.

"Instead, what the person manipulating the process discovers is all he or she got was a delay until the next meeting, or a cooling-off period. That is the antithesis of what a controller wants. No one except the controller is disturbed at the session ending early. There are other meetings scheduled and everyone will come back with a fresh attitude.

"Another thing we do," Paula continues, "is try to help get you involved in the process, Mrs. Allen. We start out by meeting in your lawyer's office so you feel more in control and in your territory. We require that you, as well as your husband, answer questions and share with us the goals and concerns you want addressed during the process. You will have an opportunity to speak to your attorney privately before, during and after the sessions.

"You both learn a new way of communicating with each other that will likely help in the future. We hear from former clients who say they now work out their issues after divorce much as we did in joint sessions. They meet at a coffee shop. The first thing they do after they sit down with coffee and a cookie is to agree on a backup date when they will meet there again if they cannot finish their task that day. Then they begin to discuss the problem, with each of them knowing that if they push too hard or too manipulatively, the other will call the meeting to an end. For many people, this adds an entirely new dynamic to their relationship. They used to just argue until one of them gave up. In that paradigm, persistence and aggression and manipulation were all rewarded. In this new paradigm, any of those tactics results in the cessation of discussion."

Understanding the Numbers

Martha looks at her quizzically. "How will I know what I'm looking at on that inventory and appraisement? I won't understand what a limited partnership interest is! I don't even know what Cedric's business is worth!"

"I can help you with that, Mom," Jeff assures her.

Paula is even more reassuring. "And we can get an

appraiser to value the interests that you feel worried about, Mrs. Allen. You don't have to just accept Cedric's values. He may have some backup documentation that satisfies you as to the value of an asset, but if he does not, then we will find you the appraiser to help you feel satisfied with the value. One of the things I am concerned about is whether you feel comfortable being in the same room with your husband and his attorney for the joint sessions. Do you?"

"Oh, yes, Cedric will be fine if you and his attorney are in the room," Martha says. "He would never want either of you to think ill of him. Not that he would be ugly to me, either, but he does get exasperated with me sometimes. But he wouldn't do that in front of you."

"Would you like to proceed with collaborative law?" asks Paula.

"I think I would," Martha answers.

"Do you want to hire me or do you have other lawyers to interview?" Paula asks.

Jeff attempts to answer, but his mother, suddenly confident, interrupts. "We do have other attorneys to interview, but I'll call you back in the next couple of days."

Paula loves collaborative law. It seems to her that it helps people just to hear about it. She is gratified that Martha seems much more empowered at the end of the meeting than at the beginning. She is pleased when Martha hires her later that week to represent her in a collaborative law divorce.

Paula and Cedric's attorney are members of a collaborative law practice group in their city, and the case proceeds much as Paula has anticipated it would. They have six joint sessions during which Cedric discloses the assets of the parties. Jeff comes to Paula's office for individual meetings with his mother and her attorney. He helps explain the financial issues to his mother in a way that she can understand and advises her on the most favorable division and distribution of those assets.

As the joint sessions progress, Martha asserts herself a little more each time. The parties divorce as civilly as they had been married. The children are able to retain their good relationship with their father and ensure that their mother is adequately compensated so that she can retain her independence.

Janet P. Brumley

12

The Large-Debt Household

K en and Linda Roberts are in the *process of divorce using collaborative law. They have been married seven years and have a 4-year-old son, Taylor. Their home is subject to a first and a second mortgage. The first lien, held by the mortgage company that loaned the purchase money for the house, is for a large sum payable over 30 years. The second lien, held by a local bank that loaned money for the installation of a pool, is for a smaller amount payable over five years. The pay-off of these two loans must be subtracted from the fair market value of the property to give a true picture of the gross equity in the home. Taylor attends a private preschool. Linda drives a new Suburban and Ken drives a new Nissan. Ken has been laid off for the past 13 months.*

> *Linda works in a business where she makes approximately $40,000 per year. Ken has become very involved in their church since his unemployment. Both recognize the other's parenting skills. They have approximately $55,000 in credit card debt, some of it accumulated by obtaining new cards for cash advances to pay the minimum balances on the earlier credit card debt.*

At the second joint session, when Ken and Linda exchange the sworn inventory and appraisement prepared by each, it becomes painfully obvious to both parties and the attorneys that, if calculated in the traditional manner of subtracting the amount of liabilities from the net value of assets, their estate will have a negative net worth.

There is some equity value in the house, despite the mortgage and the pool loan, and some value in Linda's retirement plan. But the value of the cars barely exceeds the amounts owed on them and the credit card debt is just overwhelming. Like many Americans, they live well. Most who know them would say they are people of means. It is a smoke screen we are allowed to construct in our society.

"Recognizing that your joint goals in this divorce are to protect Taylor as much as possible and allow each of you to retain your strong parental role with him," explains Linda's lawyer, George Wright, "I think we need to discuss what each of you thinks should be done about this debt."

Ken speaks up first: "I believe we should sell the house and use all the proceeds to pay off as much of our debt as possible, and then each take half of the debt and pay it off as we can."

Linda couldn't disagree more: "Well, Ken knows that I think we ought to declare bankruptcy and preserve our house proceeds to allow us each to move forward. I even made an appointment with a bankruptcy lawyer before we started the divorce and she said we were the people bankruptcy law was made to protect, but Ken was adamant that he would never do that."

"I just think it's wrong," Ken volleys. "I think the Bible teaches that we are to be responsible for our debts."

Linda counters: "And you can use your half of the house proceeds to pay on your half of the debts if you want to, but I am going to file for bankruptcy on the debts I take just as soon as the divorce is final."

"OK, let's talk a little about the law on this subject," suggests Jean Townsend, Linda's attorney. "All of your credit card debt is in both names, correct?"

"That's right," Linda and Ken chorus.

"Then if Linda files for bankruptcy on the debts she agreed to take in the divorce, the creditors will look to Ken for payment," Jean points out.

No Bankruptcy Protection

Ken's attorney offers further clarification: "Of course, we'd have the standard language in the decree confirming that Linda would hold Ken and his property harmless from the debts she is taking, and she would indemnify Ken from any liability. But the bottom line is that only bankruptcy court can relieve a debtor of a debt. A divorce decree cannot. And an indemnification from a person who's in bankruptcy is worthless. So the bottom line is that if Linda files a petition in bankruptcy, it will force Ken to do the same."

Ken is getting upset. "I was told that if Linda wanted a divorce and I didn't, then we'd get a divorce because if either one of the spouses wants a divorce, then he or she can get one. Now I'm being told that even if I don't want a bankruptcy but Linda does, then there'll be one?"

"Not necessarily," says Jean, "but if you didn't file a petition in bankruptcy yourself, you'd end up having to deal with all the debts alone."

"I can't believe this is the way the law works," Ken fumes. "She helped run those credit cards up, but now she just gets to walk away clean and I get stuck with all the debt?"

"Ken, since you don't have a job, how realistic is it to think you can pay off your share of this debt?" Linda asks.

"How does all of this impact Taylor?" Jean questions.

"If neither of us has any money from the sale of the house, " Linda says, "then we won't have money for security deposits for a rental place to live or for utilities. We'd each have to move in with our parents, and I don't think Ken would want Taylor to spend half his life with my parents. And I don't think Ken's parents would let Ken move in with them. Would they? And would that be the best situation for Taylor?"

"Of course my parents would let me move back in with them," Ken argues. "And I think that would be a fine place for Taylor to be. I do agree that Linda's parents would not be a good influence on Taylor. So maybe we're back to splitting the proceeds and splitting the debt and I'll just hope that Linda doesn't declare bankruptcy."

"I don't want to declare bankruptcy. I just don't see any other way out," Linda says.

"What if we word it so that if Linda does file a petition

in bankruptcy, she has to give notice to Ken within 24 hours and then he can make his decision whether to file at that time?" George offers.

Both parties agree that this is a good plan. There has never been any disagreement about the possession terms for Taylor. They will split time with him equally, one week on and one week off. Since Taylor attends school in the area where their house is located, however, the issue of which parent would have the right to determine domicile becomes an issue, as does the question of who will live in the house prior to its sale.

Getting Real with Ken

"How can you possibly be the person who remains in the house until its sale, Ken, when you have no income?" Linda demands.

"My parents will loan me the money," Ken replies.

"Ken, they will not. They are tapped out, between you and your sister."

"I think we'd better table the issue of who remains in the house until the next joint session, so Ken can get confirmation of whether his parents will front the expense for him," Jean says. "Linda, would you feel comfortable leaving Ken in the house if his parents agree to lend him the money?"

"Yes. If his parents agree to it, I'd be glad to get out from under it and move on. But I'll need to see something in writing from his parents agreeing to that, because Ken always thinks they'll do things they won't do," Linda answers.

"OK, so Ken will talk to his parents and bring us a letter evidencing their agreement at the next joint session, right?" George sums up.

At the next session, Ken announces that he has spoken to his parents and decided it is better to let Linda stay in the house until it sells. He will move in with his parents.

"Will you help me pay the house note?" asks Linda. "How is it fair for me to pay all the expenses there?"

"You're getting to live there," Ken responds.

George steps in: "Usually, the spouse who pays the house note gets reimbursed for the amount of principal reduction made from the date of agreement until date of closing. You usually don't get reimbursed for interest paid because you get that as a tax deduction and you usually don't get reimbursed for taxes or insurance paid because you had the benefit of living there. The two of you can make a different arrangement if you want, but that's the traditional model."

Both parties think that sounds fair. And since they know Taylor might be going to public school in the near future and Ken's parents live in an undesirable school district, Ken agrees to allow Linda to be the parent conservator with the right to determine domicile, with a geographical restriction to the desirable school district.

All of the parties' problems are not solved by collaborative law. In fact, this case shows the limitations of this method, as with all other types of divorce. It cannot create cash where there is none. They still have the big debts, but they also have a plan and an escape hatch. And perhaps more important, they have preserved their roles as involved caretakers of their child.

Janet P. Brumley

13

The Long-Term Emotionally Distant Marriage

T*he summer Mary and Herbert Walker married, she had just graduated from Southern Methodist University, which she attended while continuing to live at home with her parents. Herbert was a young attorney who had just purchased his first home. They married in Mary's home church and she literally moved from her father's house to her husband's house on her wedding day.*

Mary has never worked outside the home. Herbert never stops working. He works with a mini book light during symphony performances. He goes into his study to "catch up on his journals" each evening immediately after dinner. He leaves for work each morning at 6:15. Herbert is past retirement age but intends to keep working.

Mary's life has been her children, who are

grown when she decides to divorce. Herbert has engaged in numerous sexual affairs throughout their marriage, but these affairs did not precipitate the divorce. Mary is close to all the children, but Herbert is not. Herbert has announced that he isn't leaving one cent to any of them. When Mary questions him, Herbert tells her he is leaving everything in a trust. She will be a lifetime beneficiary. After her death, the money will go to various charities he has chosen.

The next morning, Mary makes an appointment with a divorce lawyer. She doesn't want to hurt Herbert, but she has taken care of him for a lifetime and she isn't about to let him leave everything to charities and disown their children. Of course, she is terribly concerned that she might be on her own financially, since she has never drawn a paycheck in her life. She has no idea what assets they own, but is pretty sure they have no debts other than monthly utilities and taxes.

"Are you still in love with your husband, Mrs. Walker?" asks her attorney, Glenda Anthony.

"Oh, not really. We haven't shared a bedroom in 17 years. I remember, because that's when I found out about his last affair. Since then, I haven't even tried to keep track of where he is, or why he's there. I just make his meals and wash his clothes. Otherwise, we lead separate lives."

"Have the two of you ever discussed a divorce?" Glenda prompts.

"Yes," Mary replies. "After I found out about each of his affairs, we discussed divorce, but he never wanted one. I think the reason he didn't is because he didn't want to be free to marry one of them. I think he thought one wife was trouble enough. And I didn't want to get a divorce, either. I couldn't have stood embarrassing my parents like that, but they're both dead now."

Try as she might, Glenda cannot get a good feel for why Mary wants a divorce now, other than the fact that she wants to be able to leave *her* property to her children. Glenda tries to explain that despite what Herbert says about the trust, he cannot leave her half of the community estate in the trust. Mary does not seem satisfied. When Glenda suggests that Mary might want to talk to a probate lawyer, she says she'll do that after the divorce is final and she knows what property belongs to her.

Mary likes the idea of collaborative law and takes home a brochure to show her husband.

The next day, Glenda receives a telephone call from Jim Sutton, an attorney employed by Herbert Walker. The two lawyers discuss the issues and set up the first joint session.

Trying to Control the Sessions

At the first session, the disparity of power in the relationship is obvious. Herbert Walker cannot believe he has to disclose to Mary exactly what properties they hold — including account numbers! Why, if she knows how much they have, she will become a spendthrift without a doubt! He has worked hard for this money, invested wisely. Although he is not opposed to a divorce, he simply wants to give Mary a monthly stipend for the rest of her life. Herbert tries to convince Mary this is a much more secure route for her, since no matter how much money they have, it could all be lost.

Mary is adamant. She wants property designated as hers, and hers alone, to leave to the children. And her ambitions have grown. She wants property designated as hers so she can take trips with her sister and daughter. She wants to give her grandson in college a car. She wants some money of her own and the power that goes with it.

Herbert agrees to complete a sworn inventory and appraisement and bring it, along with supporting documentation, to the next joint session. Everyone in the room is aware that Herbert knows precisely where every penny is located, but they all understand that he needs to do this in his own way.

At the next session, everyone is astounded at the size of the estate the Walkers have amassed. No one is more surprised than Mary. She says they need only to divide the estate equally and finalize the divorce.

"How is this fair?" Herbert demands. "All my adult life I've been working to amass this money and now you get to walk away with half of it. Your time has been spent amassing relationships and household knowledge. How do I get half of that? I don't know the names of my own doctors. I can't operate the washing machine. I don't know how to cook. You'll have people who will want to take care of you when you're sick, but I'll be all alone with no one."

"That's a good point," says Mary. "Who'll take care of Herbert? Can I go on living there and taking care of him? I wouldn't want people to know we were living together if we weren't married, but I guess I could come over in the mornings and cook breakfast and then leave his supper in the refrigerator."

"Do you two really want to be divorced or do you just want to split up your property?" Glenda asks.

"I don't want to do either," Herbert responds.

"I really just want to split the property. Can we do that and stay married?" Mary wonders.

Partition Agreement Possible

The two attorneys explain that in Texas, married couples may execute partition agreements (or post-marital agreements, as they are sometimes called) that divide community property assets into the husband's sole and separate property assets and the wife's sole and separate property assets. These agreements are legal documents negotiated much like the terms of a divorce decree would be negotiated. Then they are routinely followed by a declaratory judgment, so the parties have the security of hearing a court declare the validity of the partition agreement. (To find out more about these agreements, consult Chapter 16, "Post-Marital Agreements.")

After a third joint session discussing the specifics of the partition agreement and declaratory judgment, the parties agree this is the route they want to take. Glenda suggests that Mary hire a financial advisor, and she says she has already done so.

On the day they execute the partition agreement, both parties are placed under oath. They are questioned by the lawyers "on the record," which is being stenographically transcribed by a court reporter and recorded by a videographer. The next day, the parties meet at the courthouse for a prove-up of the declaratory judgment, after which they file a non-suit in their divorce action.

Their divorce turns out to be as unconventional as their marriage has been. It is not a solution most couples would welcome. There is none of the romance most people want in a marriage; their emotional distance from each other over the years has made this a marriage of convenience. But collaborative law has allowed them to craft a solution that fits them and their particular needs.

Janet P. Brumley

14

Splitting the Baby

R ob *and Patricia Powell were married
for almost 10 years before the birth of
their only child, Steffi, two years ago.
Both parents adored Steffi from the start.
Because Rob's job requires many more hours
and is more lucrative than Patricia's, she
spends much more time with Steffi and is the
little girl's primary caretaker. Patricia's strin-
gent rules and Rob's more relaxed parenting
style are sources of conflict.*

*Patricia insists that Steffi be on a rather
inflexible schedule and eat only food Patricia
has prepared and blended in the kitchen of
their own home. When Rob stays with Steffi
on occasional Saturdays so that Patricia can
enjoy a day of shopping with her sister,
Patricia often comes home to find that Steffi
has been put down for a nap at the wrong*

time, wearing dirty clothes she played in that day. Patricia feels Steffi should play indoors. Many of those days are rainy or too hot or too cold, in her opinion, for outdoor play. And certainly Steffi should have been bathed before her nap. In Patricia's opinion, babies sleep better when they are clean.

Rob sees these complaints as controlling and suffocating for Steffi. He believes children are resilient, and Steffi loves being outdoors. And he thinks that if a child doesn't sleep well at naptime, she will just make it up that night. He frequently thinks Patricia's ideas are just nuts.

Though Rob and Patricia see parenting from different viewpoints, they agree it would be in Steffi's best interest if they divorce in the least bitter manner possible.

They have chosen collaborative law as the means to achieve this.

At the first session, Rob lists as his primary goal in the process of collaborative law "to continue to be involved in Steffi's life on a 50/50 basis with her mother." Throughout the weeks of negotiation, he refuses to compromise on this point. The attorneys attempt to reframe his assertion into "continuing to be involved in Steffi's life, along with her mother," but Rob always comes back with "...on a 50/50 basis." Although Patricia is not opposed to the concept of sharing time equally at a later date, she is terrified of the idea while Steffi is so young.

"Everyone knows it's best for a child to have both parents," Rob maintains. "All I want is for her to be with her father just as much as she is with her mother."

"But Rob, she is still in diapers and a baby bed. She's just too young to be spending half her time in one place and the other half in a different place," Patricia argues.

"I know how to change diapers, and it's about time she moves into a little kid's bed, anyway. I'll get one of those with a rail on the side so she can't roll out at night."

"You work until 7 o'clock almost every night. How are you going to take care of Steffi?" asks Patricia.

"The same way you take care of her while you work," Rob answers. "I'll have Sally at my house on the days I have Steffi. And I won't work late on those days."

In Steffi's Best Interest

Patricia's attorney, Ed Simmons, chimes in. "I think I hear both of you saying you want to make sure that whatever arrangement you agree to is actually best for Steffi. Is that correct?"

Both parents agree that, of course, they want the arrangement to be handled correctly for Steffi. When Ed suggests the parties turn to a joint expert on child rearing, such as a psychologist, the idea is enthusiastically supported by Rob's attorney, Lisa James, as well.

"Frequently a psychologist can help you think of things in different and more innovative ways," Lisa joins in. "Why don't we agree to spend our next couple of joint sessions concentrating on property division and child support while the two of you visit with a psychologist for recommendations of various child possession schedules?"

The two attorneys know a number of psychologists in

the area who excel at just this sort of problem. From their years of experience, the attorneys also know which ones have a bias toward one gender or the other and which ones really play it straight. The parties agree to visit the two psychologists recommended by both of the attorneys and see if one of them is agreeable to both Rob and Patricia.

The parties attend several sessions with the psychologist they choose, both alone and together, and come back to the joint session set aside for discussion of possession times with modified attitudes.

"Dr. Lawrence told us that fathers are terribly important to daughters," Rob begins, "and that a father's attitude toward his daughter may affect her self-confidence and esteem and her relationships with other males the rest of her life."

"He also told us that he has three daughters himself and he has seen his relationship with them evolve over the years," Patricia adds. "He said that when they were really small, they preferred to spend most of their time with their mother, but now he is the soccer coach for the older two and in Indian Princesses with the youngest, and they spend about equal time with each parent, although Dr. Lawrence and his wife live together."

"So, we think we need to work out an agreement for possession that allows Steffi to spend a little more than half her time with her mom right now and steps into 50/50 when she starts school," Rob adds. "Dr. Lawrence said you two could give us some different options."

"Have you considered alternating weekends from Friday evening until Sunday evening and every Wednesday overnight for Rob's current possession?" suggests Patricia's attorney. "That would give him two consecutive nights every other week and it would assure that he never goes more than seven nights without seeing Steffi."

"Or you could split possession so that Rob has Steffi every Thursday overnight and alternate weekends. That would give Rob three consecutive nights with Steffi every other week," comments Rob's attorney.

"Why don't we do the alternate weekends and every Wednesday overnight until Steffi is 3, and then switch to every Thursday overnight and alternate weekends?" Patricia offers.

"And by the time she's 4, maybe we could extend the alternate weekends from Sunday evening until Monday morning?" Rob asks. "Then, on her 5th birthday, before she begins kindergarten, she can stay with me every Wednesday and Thursday overnight and with you every Monday and Tuesday overnight and we can alternate Friday through Sunday weekends and we'll have our 50/50 time with her."

Right of First Refusal

"That sounds OK with me," Patricia replies, "as long as I know that you're not leaving Steffi with a babysitter or your mother or someone else. I agree with Dr. Lawrence that she needs you, but I think if she isn't with you, then she needs me."

"You mean if I go out on a night that Steffi is with me, then I have to let you be the babysitter?" asks Rob. "How controlling is that? Is that nuts or is that something people do?"

"It's called a 'right of first refusal' and it is sometimes done," explains Rob's attorney. "Most people believe a child is always better off with a parent than with a non-parent.

Splitting the Baby

The key is crafting the right of first refusal so that it doesn't become overly restrictive.

"Some of the things you need to take into consideration when discussing the right of first refusal are:

- Surely you want the child to spend the night sometimes with her extended family — grandparents, aunts, cousins and the like. You just need to decide how many nights per year you think are reasonable.
- You will certainly want the child to spend the night with friends on occasion; once again, you will need to decide how many such overnights you will allow.
- At some point, each of you may remarry. Will you want the child to be required to return to the other parent if the parent in possession must be out of town on business or in the hospital, even if the child could be with her step-parent and siblings?
- At what point of absence shall the right of first refusal kick in — if the parent is absent overnight, for 24 hours, for six hours, etc.?
- How long does the responding parent have to respond affirmatively before the right is waived?"

"As you can see, this is a complex issue that will require some further discussion," Lisa says.

After talking about it, Rob and Patricia agree on a right of first refusal that becomes effective anytime the parent in possession is going to be absent for at least six hours overnight. If a parent is simply going out to eat and to a movie or getting up early and leaving on business, there is no need to offer the entire overnight to the other parent.

Also, they agree that Steffi should be allowed to spend

up to 12 overnights per year with each set of her grandparents and up to 12 overnights per year with other family members and friends, and that the right of first refusal will not become effective if Steffi will be with a step-parent and sibling, although it will remain effective until the newly married couple has a child together who would be Steffi's sibling.

With the help of the psychologist, Rob and Patricia are able to appreciate what the other's presence means to their daughter, and they craft a possession schedule that meets her needs and theirs.

15

Helping Couples
Explore Alternatives

Collaborative law is especially effective for parties who decide to explore the possibility of reconciliation or some sort of alternative form of marriage even as they pursue divorce.

The reasons for people walking this dual path are varied. In some cases, one party may be firm on the idea of divorce but may defer to the wishes of the other to at least explore ways for them to stay married. The parties may be opposed to divorce on religious grounds. Another scenario is the couple who wants to continue a family lifestyle for outward appearances while having sexual freedom or maintaining independent control over their finances. Another couple may want to divorce while protecting a spouse who has a serious pre-existing health condition that would keep him or her from replacing insurance coverage.

As you have seen in a previous scenario, with collaborative law you can divide your finances or restructure your life without actually dissolving the marriage.

Texas law allows parties two years after declaring them-selves participants in a collaborative law divorce to finalize the action. This gives plenty of time to explore alternative styles of marriage. Most people think this means reconcilia-tion. However, the alternative we most frequently see is marriage in an altered form after executing a partition agreement. The partition agreement, as executed by Mary and Herbert Walker in Chapter 13, allows parties to alter the marriage contract by redefining or recharacterizing the nature of their property.

The state of Texas has determined that all property pos-sessed during marriage is presumed to be community prop-erty. That presumption can be rebutted with clear and convincing evidence that an asset is separate property. Separate property is generally defined as property acquired prior to marriage or during marriage by gift, bequest or inheritance. Add to that definition property partitioned to one spouse by the other spouse.

Partition agreements contain language that confirms the transfer of the property as a partition, gift or exchange. The language is stilted and the form inflexible because the attor-neys want to be sure it is enforceable. A partition agreement can characterize assets in existence at the time as well as assets not yet acquired. It can make the parties as separate legally and financially as they would be after a divorce.

Some people choose to do partition agreements during their marriage to divide assets and liabilities. This may be necessary to aid in estate planning, tax planning and/or asset acquisition. In these cases, they are mere extensions of a pre-marital agreement and in no way alter the marriage rela-tionship.

However, in other cases people may choose to do partition agreements to act as a "legal divorce," while still maintaining the married facade for personal reasons.

Joshua and Jenny are at a point of no return in their marriage. The problem is Joshua's drug addiction. By the time Jenny retains an attorney to file for divorce, Joshua has checked himself into a clinic. This is the third time in their 10-year marriage that he has fought the addiction battle. Each time Jenny has stood by him. She understands it is a sickness and wants to stay married for their children's sake, but she just cannot go through the nightmare again.

"Most people think my husband is away on business," Jenny tells her attorney. "They don't know he is in the hospital and I am receiving the disconnection notices from the utility company for bills he has not paid while he was snorting coke. The children think I am a witch because I scream at Daddy when he comes home from his 'business' trips.

"My husband is a financial genius," she continues. "We have lots of money in mutual funds and stocks, but I have access to none of it. The amazing part is that he has not wasted as much money on drugs as you might think. Even when he's high, he only spends our disposable income and leaves the bills unpaid. But when he goes into the hospital, we're always out a substantial amount of money."

After Josh is released from the treatment center, he and Jenny agree to proceed collaboratively with a divorce. At the same time, they also enter counseling. They decide to enter into a partition agreement that divides all the assets on a 55/45 split in Jenny's favor. For the future, Josh agrees that his earnings during marriage will belong 50 percent to him as his sole and separate property and 50 percent to Jenny as her sole and separate property. Likewise, Jenny's earnings will belong 50 percent to her as her sole and separate property and 50 percent to Josh as his sole and separate property. Each party will contribute equally to their household expenses and be solely responsible for his or her entertainment expenses and unreimbursed medical expenses.

With this partition agreement in place, they try to reconcile their marriage. Jenny voices to all that if there is another slip in Josh's sobriety, the marriage is over.

In less than a year, Josh does lose his sobriety and ultimately they divorce using collaborative law. The only real issue in the divorce, since property has already been divided, is the children's living arrangements. Both Josh and Jenny feel the children should not have overnights with their father. Both parties agree that Josh should submit to drug testing within eight hours of any request by Jenny. Unless he can produce a clean drug test, Josh can have only supervised visits with his children. Jenny feels betrayed and Josh feels like a failure, but they both know they have done their best for their children.

16

Post-Marital Agreements

The post-marital agreement is much like a premarital agreement, or "pre-nup," except it is executed during the marriage rather than before it. Texas law allows both spouses and persons who are about to become spouses to enter into contracts that alter the treatment of property they acquire during marriage.

For instance, Angie Brown's parents are setting up a family limited partnership for estate planning purposes. Normally, disbursements from a partnership are community property in Texas. Both Angie and her husband agree that disbursements from this family limited partnership should remain Angie's separate property. To accomplish this, they will enter into a post-marital agreement. To assure the enforceability of the post-marital agreement, each of the parties must be represented by an attorney. This is to assure that Angie's husband, Tom Brown, can never claim he made the agreement out of ignorance or because he was coerced or under duress.

Agreements the Traditional Way

Because Angie knows nothing about collaborative law, she simply responds to the advice of her attorney, Charles Coleman, who only knows how to create a post-marital agreement in the traditional manner. Charles thinks that while the two of them are drafting a post-marital agreement, they should throw in other perks to her. He knows Angie's family is wealthy. Although Tom is a hard worker, he probably will never have much money.

Meanwhile, Tom's attorney, Gretchen Bergstrom, suggests that he not waive his interest in the distributions from the family limited partnership. She questions why Angie wants this done. Gretchen asks Tom if Angie is anticipating a divorce. Tom says he is sure she is not.

"I just wondered, because it won't really matter whether the distribution is separate property or community property unless you two get a divorce," Gretchen adds. Tom explains that Angie wants to make sure this property remains her separate property for their children's sake, since she considers it an inheritance from her parents.

"Oh, well, maybe that's it ..." Tom's attorney answers. "We'll see if that's really all the post-marital agreement covers when we see the first draft."

Back at Charles' office, the scenario continues to play out. "Why don't you let me just send a more standard post-marital agreement over as a first draft? It will cover a number of other issues beneficial to you as well, and if your husband really doesn't care about your money or your parents' money, he'll agree to it," Charles urges.

Angie doesn't want to be a lot of trouble and thinks the standard agreement will be just fine for her. She is really doing this more to please her family than for any other reason. They wanted her to do a premarital agreement with Tom before she married him, but she refused. She felt it was insulting to Tom, and she had no money, anyway. But now she feels she owes it to her parents, who have accumulated the money, to protect it for herself and their grandchildren.

You can guess what happens. The draft is what Tom's attorney expected. And now the comments made by both lawyers to their clients have set the stage for hurt feelings and an emotionally charged exchange. Tom is alarmed by the wide-reaching scope of the agreement and remembers his attorney's comment about the possibility of divorce. He wonders if he is being a fool. Angie was really snippy with him last week. She seems to spend more and more time with her parents, and they've never accepted him. Angie hears from her attorney that Tom is angry about the first draft and questions going forward with the agreement at all. She remembers her attorney's comment about how she'd know whether or not Tom cared about her money by the way he reacts to the agreement, and she wonders if she's been a fool all along. Is he just waiting for her parents to leave her the money?

Even if Angie and Tom are able to eventually enter into a post-marital agreement, their relationship has undergone a strain that is unnecessary.

The Collaborative Law Way

If Angie's attorney was trained in collaborative law techniques, the narrative would be different. Charles would suggest that Tom choose an attorney from the list Charles gives Angie in his office. These other attorneys are similarly trained and have a respectable level of experience and reputation, as does Charles. This approach encourages a feeling of equality at the negotiating table.

Tom chooses Gretchen Bergstrom, who calls Charles to discuss the case before they enter into their first joint session. No one gets blind-sided here. When Charles suggests he use the standard post-marital agreement that contains everything but the kitchen sink, Gretchen reminds him that their clients have stated explicitly that they want the attorneys to tailor the agreement to fit them. Tom is happy to enter into this agreement to give Angie and her parents a feeling of ease, but he might be alarmed by the extent of a standard post-marital agreement. Charles allows that Angie didn't ask for the broad scope of the standard form, but he assumed that was where they would start. However, since Gretchen seems concerned that her client might react negatively to this, Charles agrees to wait to draft the agreement until after the parties have actually discussed and agreed on the terms in joint sessions.

He points out to Gretchen that he wants to seal the deal after they have executed the post-marital agreement by doing a declaratory judgment. This is used when parties ask a judge to rule on the enforceability or provision of a contract. It is frequently used in business law to get a ruling on a non-compete agreement prior to the sale of a business, and in family law to get a ruling on a premarital agreement prior to a marriage or on a post-marital agreement prior to a disbursement or execution of some other document. It is usually a fairly simple procedure in which the parties and their attorneys make a single appearance before a judge. The parties are asked a number of questions and the judge rules on the enforceability of the document in question.

Gretchen says she thinks her client will agree to such an action, since he wants the document to be enforceable. But she suggests they bring this issue up at the next joint session, along with a discussion of sealing the records. This will prevent those who comb through public records at the courthouse from seeing and reading them.

In this scenario, the attorneys have helped the parties accomplish just what they wanted. The attorneys haven't made the situation more complicated than it needs to be. Neither attorney has obtained more or less relief for his or her client than the client wanted. In short, the attorneys stepped back and let the clients direct the course, only interjecting the lawyers' perspective and opinions when needed.

Janet P. Brumley

17

Removing the Blame Game from Family Law

One of the least productive parts of divorce is the never-ending desire of the client to recite and embellish the long list of faults and bad acts of the other side. I have never understood why a client thinks it matters in the divorce action that the husband proposed in a caddish fashion or the wife got drunk at the wedding rehearsal dinner, but almost all clients share these stories with their attorneys. Maybe it's because they are unable to differentiate between relevant and irrelevant information, or maybe they want the attorney to like them and dislike their spouse. Or perhaps it's because they feel so rejected and angry that it's helpful to remember all the negatives.

A Wretched Way to Divorce

Regardless of why divorcing people do this, it is not helpful to the settlement of the divorce action. I suspect it is not helpful in the quest to be a gracious and civil person in the midst of litigation. I also suspect they do not tell these stories only to their attorney behind a closed door and in a privileged situation. Most likely, they tell their friends, their relatives and the parents of their children's friends many of these same stories.

Invariably, the spouse hears that he or she is being disrespected with these tales and the war is on. Now the other spouse must tell all the bad stories to regain status as the wronged party. Before you know it, everyone hates everyone and they are embarrassed that all their dirty laundry has been aired to their friends and neighbors.

Children sense that parents who were only hurting from the pain of the separation are now angry and hate-filled toward the other person, who also happens to be the children's parent. The children have not only lost the two-parent home they had before the separation — they fear that if their mother can hate their father, whom she once dearly loved, perhaps she can hate them, too. They fear that if their father, always someone you could count on, could leave their mother and care nothing for her welfare, perhaps their father could quit on them, as well. Neither of these deductions is unreasonable. What the parents need to model is that even if they can no longer live together, they will always care about and want the best for the other. That would give children security at a time when they need it most.

In collaboration, you are always trying to discern what each person needs and discover how each person's needs can be met. Each person — in a divorce or not — needs to be respected and treated with dignity. It costs you nothing but an investment in integrity to give that to another human being. I use the term "investment" because that is what it is. You will get something in return.

We react to the possibility of rewards. We don't behave in a polite manner only because we are altruistically good. Many times, we do it because we understand that good social skills help us more easily get what we want and need. We treat others with respect because we have learned that only then will others accord us respect. The Golden Rule is not suspended in divorce.

It is difficult to behave graciously in the face of rejection, but it can be done and it is always a wise course. It doesn't make being rejected feel any better if you bad-mouth the one who rejected you. It seems like it would, but it really doesn't. The only thing it does is give that person license to bad-mouth you later. The blame game is like eating salted peanuts. Once you've started, you just can't stop. Once you've told your sister, you have to tell your best friend. Before you know it, everyone knows. And if you felt bad before, you feel even worse now. You've made a fool of yourself (by announcing the rejection) in front of everyone! The other person must pay.

The rejecting spouse hears the stories of perfidy and defends himself or herself with tales about you that will show why any sane person would reject you. With each telling of the tales, the rejecting spouse feels more and more validated and increasingly entitled to receive no punishment for the rejection. No one has gained. Both parties have become more entrenched and bitter toward the other.

Being A True Collaborator

True collaborators want to assist each other, keep their secrets and failures private, emphasize the positives and minimize conflict. But divorcing people who want to engage in collaboration do not engage in these actions simply because they feel compelled to "make nice." Their silence and cordiality carry a price tag. What the collaborators want for their good acts is more time with the children, more assets, more control — not to mention more self-respect and peace of mind.

Amazed friends and family talk about the couple who divorced without bitterness and seem to get along quite well with their ex-spouses, as if it is unnatural for people to be civil. But being civil beats the heck out of being the person whose secrets are discussed over dinner.

You might be thinking, "This doesn't apply to me. I don't have any secrets," but it does, and you do. You might not think of them as secrets. You might not be guilty of anything outrageous, like wearing your spouse's underwear and high heels, meeting your child's teacher for nooners at the No-Tell Motel or having a police record or a lifelong drug addiction.

But I'll bet there are things about you that you would like to keep to yourself: hanging your shirts in your closet exactly one inch apart; refusing to clean your house; obsessing over vacuum cleaner patterns on the rug; asking your wife to get an abortion; or being excessively punitive to your child as a way of teaching him a lesson. These could all qualify as behaviors you'd rather keep to yourself, and for each of these examples there are hundreds of other possibilities.

And there is no reason anyone should know. None of these things has any relevance in a divorce action. But in a litigated divorce, they could get discussed as manifestations of some personality disorder that the opposing attorney can use against you.

In collaborative law, we ask you to quit looking backward and only look toward the future. Ask yourself before you say or do anything: "Is this action or statement going to help me get nearer to the goals that I have set for this divorce?" If the answer is "No," then don't do or say it. Not for your spouse's benefit, but for your own.

18

A Call to Action: Collaborative Law for Us All

A particularly unusual feature of collaborative law is the requirement that both attorneys withdraw from a case rather than go to court if it cannot be resolved through collaborative law negotiations. This proviso confuses people and they wonder why any litigator would agree to this restriction.

Clients are not precluded from continuing the case, either through collaborative law or litigation. They simply hire another attorney. Non-lawyers find this provision contrary to conventional wisdom. They see attorneys as bottom feeders willing to do anything for money. If they give up clients willingly, don't they give up fees?

Yes, we do, but it's essential to the collaborative process. If the whole thing can come apart without agreement, then all four parties will work hard to find that agreement. Without this form of near-binding arbitration, too many divorcing parties would simply walk away when the decision-making gets difficult.

Many non-lawyers will be shocked to know that attorneys do this because many of us are are motivated by more than making money. We are human beings, believe it or not, and we want to do good and constructive work.

Not even the meanest junkyard lawyer is so greedy that he wakes up each day and says, "Boy, I wonder how many people in pain I can see today and make their lives even more miserable."

If an attorney goes to the courthouse to fight, it's because we believe we are fighting for good. We were the kids on the playground who would beat up the class bully when he picked on the class nerd. When we grew up, we recognized that talking to the bully did more good for more people more often than breaking his nose. But we still believed that right sometimes needs might, sometimes people need to be broken and sometimes hitting someone hard enough stops the fight. That's what makes litigators.

What turns litigators into collaborative law attorneys is years of searching for a way to solve a problem so it will stay solved. And the blame game clearly isn't the answer.

It is difficult at first to walk away from both the adrenaline rush and the much larger fee of litigation. But practicing collaborative law allows me to handle many more cases at once than litigation did, so that feeds my pocketbook. Also, a collaborative law practice works well with a mediator's schedule, and I enjoy mediation tremendously.

It's a new millennium, and attitudes have changed in many areas. There was a time in our not-so-distant past when people believed that a man had a right to beat his wife "with a switch no bigger than his thumb" (thus the saying "the rule of thumb"), that a parent who spared the rod spoiled the child, that the way to solve a conflict with a neighbor was to burn down his barn and that bloodlust was sport.

All over the world, people are demanding more compassionate, humane solutions to the intractable problems of human conflict. Collaborative law is simply the latest, best response to that plea in family law. Attorneys unafraid of change, who embrace learning new techniques, will be drawn to it even if they feel unable to practice it themselves. Just as surgery is not always the best medical answer, litigation is not the only legal answer. Surgeons and litigators know these things.

Growth of Collaborative Law Meets A Need

The collaborative law process, virtually unheard of just a decade ago, has grown exponentially because of the need for a more sane approach to divorce. So what does the future hold for this type of practice?

I believe we will see exactly the same progression with collaborative law that we have seen with mediation. They were both first viewed as Left Coast phenomena widely derided by Rambo practitioners as crystals-and-granola practices that are far beneath their slash-and-burn tactics — a sissy thing.

But in the end, just like with mediation, even the oldest dinosaurs will have to change and accept collaborative law or walk alone on their path to extinction. The bottom line, just as with mediation, is that it works. Just as judges demand that attorneys attempt mediation because they recognize its value, so clients will demand collaborative law because of a recognition that it is best for them.

And then, just as with mediation, civil attorneys will

claim it as their own. Collaborative law is well suited to family law, but there is no reason it cannot be used just as effectively for crafting partnership agreements, resolving differences between partners who now want to part and a myriad of other civil law situations.

Americans are, without any conscious knowledge, becoming more conditioned to solving their problems through processes. The man who leaves behind his alcohol addiction through AA, solves his cholesterol problem through a program of diet and exercise and participates in his family routine of scheduled events and task lists for his ADD or ADHD child has learned that processes solve problems.

He may not verbally describe that "working the process" has enabled him to solve problems in a more inter-active, less passive way, but he is living it. And, instinctively, just as he knows vegetables and fruits benefit his health, he knows sitting down with his former love and current enemy is the most beneficial way to resolve their conflict.

Experience tells him they cannot resolve conflict without assistance. If they could, they would not be contemplating divorce. They need a process that will secure safety for them both without putting them in the back seat while the attorneys drive them to the courthouse.

The Next Steps

I am unequivocally a believer in this new method of dispute resolution. I make no apologies about that.

It makes so much sense to me that a divorce, which is essentially a family matter, should be resolved outside the courthouse and without the undue interference of the state.

A Call to Action

Legislators who pass the laws and judges who carry them out don't love the children of this family like the parents do. Only parents have the time and patience to consider all the possible alternatives and the consequences of each alternative for their children. For everyone at the courthouse, it is just a day at work. For parents, it is the world of their children — a world the parents want to make as safe and comfortable as possible.

The same concern goes for suits involving the modification of child custody and visitation as well as premarital and post-marital agreements. The latter, it seems to me, necessitate some businesslike thinking, but should not be adversarial. Just as a couple faces numerous other decisions with differing perspectives — children or no children, house or condominium, vacation fund or retirement supplemental fund, — the negotiation of a premarital or post-marital agreement should be seen as the first test of how capable they are of hearing each other's concerns and crafting a solution acceptable to both. It should not be a hardball, "my way or the highway" presentation, but rather a good-faith negotiation of each person's interests and fears.

If you decide to approach your need through collaborative law, this is where you go from here:

First, find an attorney trained in collaborative law. This book lists by city every collaboratively trained attorney in Texas. More are being trained each day, so I don't guarantee that this is a comprehensive list. You can also search the World Wide Web. Using Google, MSN, Yahoo or one of the other major search engines, type in "collaborative law" + divorce + [name of your city or state]. This should net you a number of links to law firms and other sites dealing with collaborative law divorce.

When you interview an attorney, ask how many cases he or she has handled collaboratively and how many trainings he or she has completed. This shouldn't be the determining factor for you in hiring or not hiring the attorney. What you really want is someone who makes you feel he or she is going to assist you in your laudable goal of dignity and honesty for the sake of preserving your reputation, your children, your relationships and your estate. What you don't want is someone to pick your pocket while picking a fight. After the interview, if you feel comfortable with this attorney, hire that person.

If you do not feel comfortable with the attorney, do not sign anything. That's the rule, no matter how smart the attorney may be or how highly that person is recommended. Divorce is an emotional experience. You do not need the added stress of an attorney you don't like or, worse yet, don't trust. Remember, in this process you don't want an attorney who says flattering things about you and insults your spouse. That might make you feel better in the short term, but it is appealing to your lower-functioning self and is not beneficial in the long run. Just as you pick a personal trainer who will make you work out even when you don't feel like it, you want a collaborative lawyer who will encourage you to act in ways that are beneficial to you in the long run, even if they don't feel as good right now. You don't hide behind a collaborative attorney. You walk shoulder-to-shoulder. You are an active participant in this major event in your life.

The best attorney for another person might not be the best attorney for you. For instance, you may have a busy schedule and want to be able to fire off an e-mail to your attorney and get a brief but prompt response. Another person may want an attorney who will sit and chat about an issue. One attorney is not necessarily better than the other, just different. As we said before in this book, collaborative law is all about "one size does not fit all." You get to choose the lawyer who most closely fits your style. I hope you have a good experience that helps alleviate the stress, pain, embarrassment and damage often encountered.

If you choose the collaborative process, please write to me (at the address on the title page at the beginning of the book) and let me know how it worked for you. This is still a new process, and I want to know how it works with clients and attorneys across the state.

Thank you for wanting to act civilly when you hurt the most, salvaging a long-term relationship it would be easy to trash and recognizing that acting politely is always in your self-interest.

Many of us learned civil behavior in kindergarten. We just forgot it in a society where the assertive crow over those who compromise and the accommodating are portrayed as wimps. You don't have to teach your spouse a lesson. You don't have to be arbitrary for the principle of the thing. You don't have to prove to anyone, least of all yourself, that this is not your fault. All you have to do is walk your path with as much grace as possible.

Texas Collaborative Lawyer Directory And Appendices

All appendix items provided with permission from the Dallas Alliance of Collaborative Family Lawyers: www.dallascollaborativelaw.com

Janet P. Brumley

Dallas Alliance Of Collaborative Family Lawyers

Jimmy L. Verner, Jr. is a partner at Verner & Brumley. He graduated from Emory University with a master's degree in political science and received his J.D. from the University of San Diego. He is a frequent writer and lecturer for the State Bar of Texas and the editor of a family law newsletter. Jimmy is board certified in both civil trial and family law by the Texas Board of Legal Specialization and a member of the Texas Academy of Family Law Specialists.

Thomas L. Raggio is a past chair of the family law section of the State Bar of Texas and a fellow in the American Academy of Matrimonial Lawyers. He is board certified in family law by the Texas Board of Legal Specialization and is a member of the Texas Academy of Family Law Specialists. Tommy received his J.D. from Southern Methodist University and was one of the founding members of the Dallas Alliance of Collaborative Family Lawyers.

Thomas C. Railsback received his J.D. from Southern Methodist University and is board certified in family law by the Texas Board of Legal Specialization. He is a member of the Texas Academy of Family Law Specialists and is trained as a mediator.

William B. Pasley received his J.D. from Southern Methodist University and is board certified in family law by the Texas Board of Legal Specialization. He is a member of the Texas Academy of Family Law Specialists.

George M. Parker received his J.D. from Southern Methodist University and is board certified in family law by the Texas Board of Legal Specialization. He is a member of the Texas Academy of Family Law Specialists and a past president of the Collin County Bar Association.

Dallas Alliance of Collaborative Family Lawyers

Kathryn J. Murphy received her J.D. from Southern Methodist University and is board certified in family law by the Texas Board of Legal Specialization. She is a member of the Texas Academy of Family Law Specialists and a frequent writer and lecturer for the State Bar of Texas. She is co-author of the *Texas Family Law Practice Guide* from West Publishing. Kathryn serves on the grievance committee of the State Bar of Texas.

Robert J. Matlock received his J.D. from the University of Texas and is board certified in family law by the Texas Board of Legal Specialization. He is a member of the Texas Academy of Family Law Specialists. Bob is trained as a mediator and is active in alternative dispute resolution.

John V. McShane received his J.D. from the University of Texas and is board certified in criminal law and family law by the Texas Board of Legal Specialization. He is a member of the Texas Academy of Family Law Specialists and a frequent writer and lecturer for the State Bar of Texas. John has served on the grievance committee of the State Bar. He is one of two members who participated in the collaborative law training in California in 1999 and brought it to Texas in 2000. John was one of the founding members of the Dallas Alliance of Collaborative Family Lawyers.

Mary Johanna McCurley received her J.D. from St. Mary's University of San Antonio and is board certified in family law by the Texas Board of Legal Specialization. She is a frequent writer and lecturer for the State Bar of Texas. She is a member of the Texas Academy of Family Law Specialists, a fellow in the American Academy of Matrimonial Lawyers, a past president of the Texas Chapter of American Academy of Matrimonial Lawyers and the family law section of the State Bar of Texas. Mary Jo has also served on the board of governors and the grievance committee for the State Bar of Texas.

Kelly McClure received her J.D. from St. Mary's

Janet P. Brumley

University of San Antonio and is board certified in family law by the Texas Board of Legal Specialization. She is a member of the Texas Academy of Family Law Specialists and was one of the founding members of the Dallas Alliance of Collaborative Family Lawyers.

Paula Larsen received her J.D. from Rutgers University and is board certified in family law by the Texas Board of Legal Specialization. She is a member of the Texas Academy of Family Law Specialists and a fellow in the American Academy of Matrimonial Lawyers. Paula is a frequent writer and lecturer for the State Bar of Texas and has served on the board of governors and the grievance committee for the State Bar of Texas. She has served as both an associate judge and a district judge in Dallas County, Texas, and is trained as a mediator. Paula was one of the founding members of the Dallas Alliance of Collaborative Family Lawyers.

Jody L. Johnson received her J.D. from Southern Methodist University and is board certified in family law by the Texas Board of Legal Specialization. She is a member of the Texas Academy of Family Law Specialists and has served on the grievance committee of the State Bar of Texas. She has also served as a volunteer associate judge for the Dallas County Family Law Courts.

Douglas Harrison received his J.D. from Southern Methodist University. He is new to collaborative law and enthusiastic about its application.

Larry Hance received his J.D. from Southern Methodist University and is board certified in family law by the Texas Board of Legal Specialization. He is a member of the Texas Academy of Family Law Specialists and a frequent writer and lecturer for the State Bar of Texas. Larry has served on the grievance committee of the State Bar of Texas. He is one of two members who participated in the collaborative law training in California in 1999 and brought it to Texas. Larry is one of the

Dallas Alliance of Collaborative Family Lawyers

founding members of the Dallas Alliance of Collaborative Family Lawyers.

Kevin R. Fuller received his J.D. from Baylor University and is board certified in family law by the Texas Board of Legal Specialization. He is a member of the Texas Academy of Family Law Specialists and a frequent writer and lecturer for the State Bar of Texas.

Edwin W. Davis received his J.D. from Southern Methodist University and is board certified in family law by the Texas Board of Legal Specialization. He is a member of the Texas Academy of Family Law Specialists and a frequent writer and lecturer for the State Bar of Texas. He is also a certified public accountant.

Gay G. Cox received her J.D. from Southern Methodist University and is board certified in family law by the Texas Board of Legal Specialization. She is a member of the Texas Academy of Family Law Specialists. She is trained as a mediator and is active in alternative dispute resolution. Gay was one of the founding members of the Dallas Alliance of Collaborative Family Lawyers.

Carla Calabrese received her J.D. from the University of Cincinnati. She is a member of the American Academy of Adoption Attorneys and is trained as a mediator.

Paul Brumley is my husband and partner. He received his J.D. from Baylor University and is board certified in family law by the Texas Board of Legal Specialization. Paul is a member of the Texas Academy of Family Law Specialists and is trained as a mediator.

Angeline Lindley Bain received her J.D. from Southern Methodist University and is board certified in family law by the Texas Board of Legal Specialization. She is a member of the Texas Academy of Family Law Specialists and a fellow in the American Academy of Matrimonial Lawyers. Angie is a frequent writer and lecturer for the State Bar of Texas and has served on both the board of governors and the grievance committee for the State Bar. She has also served as an associate judge in Dallas County, Texas, and is trained as a mediator. Angie was one of the founding members of the Dallas Alliance of Collaborative Family Lawyers.

Leota Heil Alexander received her J.D. from Texas Tech University and is board certified in family law by the Texas Board of Legal Specialization. She is a member of the Texas Academy of Family Law Specialists and is a frequent writer and lecturer for the State Bar of Texas. Leota has served on the grievance committee for the State Bar and was one of the founding members of Dallas Alliance of Collaborative Family Lawyers.

Texas Family Lawyers
Trained in Collaborative Law
(as of September 15, 2003)

Note: This list was compiled from available sources. There is no guarantee as to the accuracy of this information, including addresses and telephone numbers. Most attorneys in private practice who have undergone collaborative law training are listed in the phone book, so we suggest you start there if you find an incorrect number on the list.

ADDISON

Camille Cooper Scroggins
Of Counsel, Allison & Johnson, LLP
5000 Legacy Dr., Suite 160, Plano, TX 75024
(972) 608-8905

ARLINGTON

Karen Cushman
2408-A Garden Park Ct., Arlington, TX 76013
(817) 794-5851

Stephanie Foster
4214 Little Rd., Suite 1000, Arlington, TX 76016
(817) 277-2805

Matthew Riek
2216 S. Cooper, Arlington, TX 76013
(817) 276-6000

Carol Spracklen
722 N. Fielder, Arlington, TX 76012
(817) 275-4087

AUSTIN

Kristen Algert
Ausley, Algert, Robertson & Flores, LLP
3307 Northland Dr., Suite 420, Austin, TX 78731
(512) 454-8791

James L. Arth
700 Lavaca, Suite 1150, Austin, TX 78701
(512) 479-8989

Thomas Ausley
Ausley, Algert, Robertson & Flores, LLP
3307 Northland Dr., Suite 420, Austin, TX 78731
(512) 454-8791

Kelly Ausley-Flores
Ausley, Algert, Robertson & Flores, LLP
3307 Northland Dr., Suite 420, Austin, TX 78731
(512) 454-8791

Martin Boozer
2705 Bee Caves Rd., Suite 240
Austin, TX 78746
(512) 477-5448

Carolyn Collins
611 W. 14th St., Austin, TX 78701
(512) 474-4704

Collaborative Lawyer Directory

Patricia A. English
Noelke, English & Prescott, LLP
700 Lavaca, Suite 930, Austin, TX 78701
(512) 480-9777

Philip C. Friday, Jr.
700 Lavaca, Suite 1150, Austin, TX 78701
(512) 472-9291

Amy K. Gehm
Law Offices of Jennifer Tull
506 W. 7th St., Austin, TX 78701
(512) 476-1806

Diane Hebner
Law Office of Diane Hebner
507 W. 7th St., Austin, TX 78701
(512) 477-4158

Leslie D. Hume
703 W. 10th St., Austin, TX 78701
(512) 469-9574

Mary E. Jones
703 W. 10th St., Austin, TX 78701
(512) 469-9574

Keith D. Maples
2705 Bee Caves Rd., Suite 240, Austin, TX 78746
(512) 477-5448

Catherine A. Mauzy
700 Lavaca, Suite 1150, Austin, TX 78701
(512) 474-1493

Bendolyn Johncy Mundo
8406 Spring Valley Dr., Austin, TX 78736
(512) 288-6699

Lea Noelke
Noelke, English & Prescott, LLP
700 Lavaca, Suite 930, Austin, TX 78701
(512) 480-9777

Eric Robertson
Ausley, Algert, Robertson & Flores, LLP
3307 Northland Dr., Suite 420, Austin, TX 78731
(512) 454-8791

Amie Rodnick
Law Office of Amie Rodnick
507 W. 7th St., Austin, TX 78701
(512) 477-2226

Jennifer Scates
5750 Balcones Dr., Suite 207, Austin, TX 78731
(512) 407-8228

Larry Paul Schaubhut, Jr.
4611 Bee Caves Rd., Suite 302, Austin, TX 78746-5284
(512) 330-9656

William R. Travis
507 W. 10th St., Austin, TX 78701
(512) 476-9002

Jennifer Tull
506 W. 7th St., Austin, TX 78701
(512) 472-1806

Collaborative Lawyer Directory

J. Tim Whitten
316 W. 12th St., Suite 311, Austin, TX 78701
(512) 478-1011

Melissa Williams
2705 Bee Caves Rd., Suite 240, Austin, TX 78746
(512) 477-5448

Wade Armstrong Wilson
609 W. 9th St., Austin, TX 78701
(512) 473-8373

BASTROP

Robert E. Jenkins, Jr.
Kershaw & Jenkins
Box 547, Bastrop, TX 78602
(512) 303-4700

BAY CITY

B. Allen Cumbie
1514 7th St., Bay City, TX 77414
(979) 245-1623

BAYTOWN

Myrna J. Dunnam
503 Ward Rd., Baytown, TX 77520
(281) 422-8777

BEDFORD

Anita Cutrer
1901 Central Dr., Suite 500, Bedford, TX 76021
(817) 283-3999

Janet Denton
1901 Central Dr., Suite 500, Bedford, TX 76021
(817) 283-3999

Lisa Hoppes
1901 Central Dr., Suite 500, Bedford, TX 76021
(817) 283-3999

Sid Shapiro
405 Airport Freeway, Suite 1, Bedford, TX 76021
(817) 410-4696

Diane Wanger
304 Harwood Rd., Bedford, TX 76021
(817) 268-1711

BEEVILLE

Boyd Bauer
Bauer & Bauer
P.O. Box 1436, Beeville, TX 78104
(361) 358-0475

BOERNE

Mike Jackson
14310 Northbrook, Suite 210, San Antonio, TX 78232
(210) 348-9600

BRYAN

Honorable John Delaney
Senior District Judge
43213 Birchcrest Ln., Bryan, TX 77802
(979) 219-1100

Anne Cofer
Cofer & Cofer, Inc.
P.O. Box 3520, Bryan, TX 77805
(979) 822-7575

Linda Meekins McLain
Rodgers, Miller & McLain, PC
4444 Carter Creek Pkwy, Suite 208, Bryan, TX 77805
(979) 260-9911

COLLEYVILLE

Don Teller
4005 Gateway Dr., Suite 250, Colleyville, TX 76034
(817) 267-7411

CONROE

Margaret Alexander
428 N. Main St., Conroe, TX 77301
(936) 756-4554

DALLAS

Sherrie R. Abney
2840 Keller Springs Rd., Suite 204, Carrollton, TX 75006
(972) 788-0252

Leota H. Alexander
Leota H. Alexander, PC
5910 N. Central, Suite 1475, Dallas, TX 75206
(214) 987-2191

Sylvia Atkins
8117 Preston Rd., Suite 300, Dallas, TX 75225
(214) 346-9550

Angeline Lindley Bain
Goranson, Bain & Larsen, LC
8150 N. Central, Suite 1850, Dallas, TX 75206
(214) 373-7676

Ann Turner Beletic
2929 Carlisle, Suite 170, Dallas, TX 75204
(214) 953-0017

George Bienfang
McShane, Davis & Hance, LLP
2651 N. Harwood St., Suite 350, Dallas, TX 75201
(214) 969-7300

Jon R. Boyd
Boyd & Boyd, LLP
17300 Dallas Pkwy, Suite 3160, Dallas, TX 75248
(214) 750-5055

Bill Branson
3198 Royal Ln., Suite 210, Dallas, TX 75229
(214) 350-3588

Collaborative Lawyer Directory

Janet P. Brumley
Verner & Brumley, PC
3131 Turtle Creek Blvd., Suite 1020, Dallas, TX 75219
(214) 526-5234

Paul Brumley
Verner & Brumley, PC
3131 Turtle Creek Blvd., Suite 1020, Dallas, TX 75219
(214) 526-5234

R.C. Bunger
P.O. Box 670959, Dallas, TX 75367
(972) 991-8787

Sandra Burns
Preston Commons-West 300
8117 Preston Rd., Dallas, TX 75225
(972) 601-2176

Carla M. Calabrese
Calabrese Associates, PC
311 N. Market St., Suite 300, Dallas, TX 75202
(214) 939-3000

Gay G. Cox
2213 Boll St., Dallas, TX 75204
(214) 522-0150

Edwin W. Davis
McShane & Davis, LLP
2651 N. Harwood St., Suite 350, Dallas, TX 75201
(214) 969-7300

Suzanne Mann Duvall
4080 Stanford Ave., Dallas, TX 75225
(214) 361-0802

Melinda Eitzen
McClure, Duffy & Eitzen
5000 Legacy Dr., Suite 160, Plano, TX 75024
(972) 403-1200

Barbara Elias-Perciful
3611 Fairmount, Dallas, TX 75219
(214) 522-7880

Melinda Fagin
311 N. Market St., Suite 300, Dallas, TX 75202
(214) 761-1999

Joey Fox
2501 Oak Lawn Ave., Suite 350 Dallas, TX 75219
(214) 631-1776

Andrea Hillard Frye
100 N. Central, Suite 506, Dallas, TX 75201
(214) 752-1540

Kevin R. Fuller
Koons, Fuller, VandenEykel & Robertson
2311 Cedar Springs, Suite 300, Dallas, TX 75201
(214) 871-2727

K. Dennise Garcia
8144 Walnut Hill Ln., Suite 1080, Dallas, TX 75231
(214) 739-8900

Collaborative Lawyer Directory

Thomas Greenwald
Goranson, Bain & Larsen
8150 N. Central, Suite 1850, Dallas, TX 75206
(214) 373-7676

Larry Hance
Hance & Associates
5420 LBJ Freeway, Suite 626, Dallas, TX 75240
(469) 374-9600

Honorable Frances Ann Harris
302nd District Court
Allen Courts Building, 5th Floor
600 Commerce St., Dallas, TX 75202
(214) 653-3375

Douglas Harrison
Gardere Wynne Sewell, LLP
1601 Elm St., 27th Floor, Dallas, TX 75201
(214) 999-4614

Lori Chrisman Hockett
2313 Boll St., Dallas, TX 75204
(214) 999-0800

Jim Hunt
14027 Coit Rd., Dallas, TX 75240
(972) 392-2500

Terrie Jenevein
2900 Daniel Ave., Dallas, TX 75205
(214) 368-1200

Paula Larsen
Goranson, Bain & Larsen, LC
8150 N. Central, Suite 1850, Dallas, TX 75206
(214) 373-7676

Honorable Andrew D. Leonie
IV-D Master
George L. Allen, Sr. Courts Building
600 Commerce St., Room 4108, Dallas, TX 75202

Honorable Marilea Lewis
600 Commerce St., Suite 529, Dallas, TX 75202
(214) 653-7207

Shannon R. Lynch
8117 Preston Rd., Suite 800, Dallas, TX 75225
(214) 696-3200

Kelly McClure
McClure, Duffee & Eitzen, LLP
8115 Preston Rd., Suite 270, Dallas, TX 75225
(214) 692-8200

Mary Johanna McCurley
McCurley, Orsinger, McCurley & Nelson, LLP
5950 Sherry Ln., Suite 800, Dallas, TX 75225
(214) 273-2400

John V. McShane
McShane & Davis, LLP
2651 N. Harwood St., Suite 350, Dallas, TX 75201
(214) 969-7300

Collaborative Lawyer Directory

Bonnie Marsteller
5001 LBJ Freeway, Suite 700, Dallas, TX 75244
(972) 233-3645

Robert J. Matlock
12221 Merit Dr., Suite 1660, Dallas, TX 75251
(972) 387-9955

Lawrence R. Maxwell
8226 Douglas Ave., Suite 550, Dallas, TX 75225
(214) 265-9668

Diana Meier
Goranson, Bain & Larsen, LC
8150 N. Central, Suite 1850, Dallas, TX 75206
(214) 373-7676

Michael L. Meripolski
11325 Pegasus, Suite W-211, Dallas, TX 75238
(214) 341-7765

Deborah Slye Miller
Miller, Shelton & Pace
4514 Cole Ave., Suite 525; LB 42, Dallas, TX 75205
(214) 559-6173

Frank Moore
Moore, Vrana & Padgitt
4144 N. Central Expwy, Suite 1200, Dallas, TX 75204
(214) 369-8596

Joseph O'Brien
Legal Services of North Texas
1515 Main St., Dallas, TX 75201
(214) 748-1234

Polly O'Toole
8117 Preston Rd., Suite 300, Dallas, TX 75225
(214) 346-9550

J. Durrell Padgitt
Moore, Vrana & Padgitt
4144 N. Central, Suite 1200, Dallas, TX 75204
(214) 369-8596

Steve Palmer
Palmer, Allen & McTaggart, LLP
8111 Preston Rd., Suite 300, Dallas, TX 75225-6308
(214) 265-0069

William B. Pasley
Law Offices of William B. Pasley
2911 Turtle Creek Blvd., Suite 1200, Dallas, TX 75219
(214) 520-7494

Lawrence J. Praeger
2608 State St., Dallas, TX 75204
(214) 871-0700

Irv W. Queal
8117 Preston Rd., Suite 800, Dallas, TX 75225
(214) 696-3200

Thomas C. Railsback
Robertson & Railsback
705 Ross Ave., Dallas, TX 75202
(214) 748-9211

Collaborative Lawyer Directory

Thomas L. Raggio
Raggio & Raggio, PLLC
3316 Oak Grove, Suite 100, Dallas, TX 75204
(214) 880-7500

Elisa Reiter
8226 Douglas Ave., Suite 550, Dallas, TX 75225
(214) 219-9800

Holly A. Schymik
4655 N. Central, Suite 101, Dallas, TX 75205-4022
(214) 526-9966

Myrna Silver
8950 N. Central, Suite 130, Dallas, TX 75231
(214) 365-0050

Bud Silverberg
Silverberg Mediation Services
13355 Noel Rd., Suite 500, Dallas, TX 75240
(972) 628-3737

Georganna Simpson
1349 Empire Central Dr., Suite 600, Dallas, TX 75247
(214) 905-3739

Andrea Stoller
8117 Preston Rd., Suite 300, Dallas, TX 75225
(214) 706-9076

Barbara Van Duyne
Raggio & Raggio, PLLC
3316 Oak Grove Ave., Dallas, TX 75204
(214) 880-7500

Jimmy L. Verner, Jr.
Verner & Brumley, PC
3131 Turtle Creek Blvd., Suite 1020, Dallas, TX 75219
(214) 526-5234

Beverly Ward Via
8117 Preston Rd., Suite 800, Dallas, TX 75225
(214) 696-3200

Susan Vrana
Moore, Vrana & Padgitt
4144 N. Central, Suite 1200, Dallas, TX 75204
(214) 369-8596

Lynn Davis Ward
Ward, O'Brien
1080 Walnut Glen Tower
8144 Walnut Hill Ln., Dallas, TX 75231-4344
(214) 739-8900

Clint Westhoff
McClure Duffee & Eitzen, LLP
8115 Preston Rd., Suite 270, Dallas, TX 75225
(214) 890-2754

Jana Wickham
Hance & Associates
5420 LBJ Freeway
2 Lincoln Center, Suite 626, Dallas, TX 75240
(469) 374-9600

Jenny Womack
Calabrese Associates
311 N. Market St., Suite 300, Dallas, TX 75202
(214) 939-3000

DENTON

Jonita Boyd Borchardt
101 N. Elm, Suite 201-B, Denton, TX 76201
(940) 387-2203

Davis S. Bouschor, II
217 E. Oak St., Denton, TX 76201
(940) 323-1300

Mike Gregory
303 N. Carroll, Suite 100, Denton, TX 76209
(940) 387-1600

Darcy Loveless
Loveless & Loveless
218 N. Elm, Denton, TX 76201
(940) 387-3776

S. Camille Milner
620 W. Hickory St., Denton, TX 76201
(940) 383-2674

EL CAMPO

Karen Meinardus
411 W. Jackson, El Campo, TX 77437
(979) 543-6822

EL PASO

Gary A. Aboud
400 E. Overland, El Paso, TX 79901
(915) 532-2480

Honorable Kathleen Anderson
Family Court II
500 E. San Antonio, Suite 1102, El Paso, TX 79901
(915) 543-3871

M. Daisy Everhart
718 Myrtle Ave., El Paso, TX 79901
(915) 533-7216

Carmen B. Hegeman
1700 N. Stanton, El Paso, TX 79902
(915) 532-3638

Paul J. Kubinski
10514 Montwood Dr., El Paso, TX 79935
(915) 593-8883

C. Jeff Minor
2211 E. Missouri, #N-310, El Paso, TX 79903
(915) 532-7200

Gregory B. Pine
303 Texas, #1000, El Paso, TX 79901
(915) 532-5757

Heather Ronconi
4157 Rio Bravo, El Paso, TX 79902
(915) 532-7005

Collaborative Lawyer Directory

Felix Saldivar, Jr.
3160 Lee Trevino, #110-A
El Paso, TX 79936
(915) 590-9500

Gene Semko
2211 E. Missouri, #N-310, El Paso, TX 79903
(915) 532-7200

Douglas C. Smith
10514 Montwood Dr., El Paso, TX 79935
(915) 593-6600

Paula Thomas
615 E. Schuster, Suite 10, El Paso, TX 79902
(915) 533-9955

Susan Urbieta
521 Texas Ave., El Paso, TX 79901
(915) 544-9061

Frederick X. Walker
9531 Dyer St., El Paso, TX 79924
(915) 755-1336

Donald Williams
3301 Rain Dance Dr., El Paso, TX 79936
(915) 592-4011

FORT WORTH

Vaughn Bailey
1209 E. Belknap St., Fort Worth, TX 76102
(817) 877-3166

Janet P. Brumley

Bill E. Bowers
1320 S. University Dr., Suite 825, Fort Worth, TX 76107
(817) 332-9640

Bob Bowland
5155 Wichita St., Fort Worth, TX 76119
(817) 535-2859

Raymond Daniel
5009 Brentwood Stair Rd., Suite 102, Fort Worth, TX 76103
(817) 446-3360

Michelle Evans
1701 River Run, Suite 1118, Fort Worth, TX 76112
(817) 335-5455

David Flores
1512 8th Ave., Suite 500, Fort Worth, TX 76104
(817) 924-2889

Kathryn Laws
1201 E. Belknap, Fort Worth, TX 76102
(817) 336-3033

Cynthia McKenzie
221 W. Exchange Ave., Suite 204, Fort Worth, TX 76106
(817) 877-4000

Zoe Meigs
One Summit Ave., Suite 208, Fort Worth, TX 76102
(817) 336-2325

Collaborative Lawyer Directory

Lynne Milford
2630 W. Freeway, Suite 218, Fort Worth, TX 76102
(817) 877-3394

Dick Price
307 W. 7th St., Suite 1905, Fort Worth, TX 76102
(817) 338-4633

Andrew Stasio
303 Main St., Suite 302, Fort Worth, TX 76102
(817) 332-5113

Alan J. Weast
115 N. Henderson St., Fort Worth, TX 76102
(817) 870-1974

John P. White
400 E. Weatherford, Fort Worth, TX 76102
(817) 334-0747

Douglas Wright
3265 Lackland Rd., Fort Worth, TX 76116
(817) 738-4940

GALVESTON

Emily A. Fisher
Martin, Garza, Fisher & Lanan, LLP
1100 Rosenberg, Galveston, TX 77550
(409) 765-5705

GEORGETOWN

Chris Mealy
P.O. Box 326, Georgetown, TX 78627
(512) 948-8008

GRAPEVINE

Jon Michael Franks
128 E. Texas St., Suite 100, Grapevine, TX 76051
(817) 329-5573

HARKER HEIGHTS

Fancy Jezek
Holbrook & Hezek
P.O. Box 2548, Harker Heights, TX 76548
(254) 690-2202

HELOTES

Ron Bird
Bird & Noll
P.O. Box 169, Helotes, TX 78023
(210) 695-9992

HOUSTON

Steven Abramowitz
11 Greenway Plaza
2121 Summit Tower, Houston, TX(
(713) 623-6700

Collaborative Lawyer Directory

Elizabeth Asher
2401 Fountainview, Suite 622, Houston, TX 77057
(713) 974-0650

Steve A. Bavousett
One Riverway, Suite 1820, Houston, TX 77056
(713) 871-9587

Cynthia Behelfer
2727 Allen Pkwy., Suite 1800, Houston, TX 77019
(713) 728-0100

Renee Beilue
Beilue & Stewart, PC
1080 W. Sam Houston Pkwy N., #114, Houston, TX 77024
(713) 465-7177

John Bock
440 Louisiana, Suite 440, Houston, TX 77002
(713) 739-0902

Bret A. Bosker
Maureen Peltier & Associates, PC
952 Echo Ln., Suite 422, Houston, TX 77024
(713) 461-5288

Martha Bourne
1177 W. Loop S., Suite 650, Houston, TX 77027
(713) 961-9663

Jennifer A. Broussard
3816 W. Alabama, Suite 205, Houston, TX 77027
(713) 840-9017

Fran Brochstein
8980 Kirby Dr., Houston, TX 77054
(713) 847-6000

Carol Callaway
1010 Lamar St., Suite 450, Houston, TX 77002
(713) 655-0300

David L. Capps
12337 Jones Rd., Suite 102, Houston, TX 77070
(281) 469-2204

Bernard Chanon
Ducoff & Chanon
3306 Mercer, Houston, TX 77027
(713) 961-3701

Bill Connolly
2930 Revere, Suite 300, Houston, TX 77098
(713) 520-5757

Sherri Cothrun
917 Franklin, Suite 220, Houston, TX 77002
(713) 228-2858

Vonda Covington
3730 Kirby Dr., Suite350, Houston, TX 77098
(713) 773-4909

Michael Craig
1177 W. Loop South, Suite 650, Houston, TX 77027
(713) 627-8991

Collaborative Lawyer Directory

Beth Dickson (Divorce Planner)
Equitable Solutions, Inc.
50 Briar Hollow, Suite 120-W, Houston, TX 77027
(713) 599-1220

Judy Dougherty
909 Kipling, Houston, TX 77006
(713) 521-9551

Jack H. Emmott, III
5120 Woodway, Suite 10002, Houston, TX 77056
(713) 840-1300

Barbara Epperson
5120 Woodway, Suite 10002, Houston, TX 77056
(713) 840-1300

Melissa Fertel
2727 Allen Pkwy., Suite 1800, Houston, TX 77019
(713) 524-2453

Rhoda Forbes-Kirk
9521 Westheimer, Suite 378, Houston, TX 77063
(713) 952-3027

Kathleen Gasner
3816 W. Alabama, Suite 105, Houston, TX 77027
(713) 224-5400

Marilyn Golub
6750 W. Loop South, Suite 500, Bellaire, TX 77401
(713) 743-5462

Don West Graul
2930 Revere, Suite 300, Houston, TX 77098
(713) 629-1416

Liza A. Greene
9610 Long Point, Suite 130, Houston, TX 77055
(713) 365-9315

Carol Griffin
Maureen Peltier & Associates
952 Echo Lane, Suite 422, Houston, TX 77024
(713) 461-5288

Ellen Elkins Grimes
2727 Allen Pkwy., Suite 1800, Houston, TX 77019
(713) 524-2453

Elena Halachian-Kritzer
13301 E. Freeway, Suite 210, Houston, TX 77015
(713) 455-8851

Pamela Halliburton
1111 Fannin, Suite 1370, Houston, TX 77007
(713) 759-6931

Honorable Bonnie Hellums
1115 Congress, Houston, TX 77003
(713) 755-6246

Michael A. Hiller
11 Greenway Plaza, Suite 2810, Houston, TX 77046
(713) 977-8686

Collaborative Lawyer Directory

Heather Hughes
Tindall & Foster, PC
1300 Post Oak Blvd., Suite 2200, Houston, TX 77056
(713) 622-8733

Sheryl B. Johnson
2939 Ferndale, Houston, TX 77098
(713) 528-5252

Sondra Kaighen
17049 El Camino Real, Suite 201, Houston, TX 77058
(281) 488-1918

Patricia Lasher
The Fullenweider Firm
4265 San Felipe, Suite 1400, Houston, TX 77027
(713) 624-4100

Beverly B. Lord
3816 W. Alabama, Suite 222, Houston, TX 77027
(713) 961-9660

Julia Lovorn
12777 Jones Rd., Suite 475, Houston, TX 77065
(281) 469-2922

Kathryn Marteeny
11767 Katy Frwy., Suite 740, Houston, TX 77079
(713) 961-0000

Karen McKay
550 Westcott, Suite 350, Houston, TX 77007
(713) 880-4691

Connie Moore
3608 Audubon, Houston, TX 77006
(713) 522-4282

Bradford E. Morris
402 Main, 7th Floor, Houston, TX 77002
(713) 228-1515

William W. Morris
3040 Post Oak Blvd., Suite 1300, Houston, TX 77056
(713) 552-1234

Steven W. Ongert
Dean & Ongert, PC
16808 El Camino Real, Houston, TX 77058
(281) 486-8125

Imogen S. Papadopoulos
4265 San Felipe, Suite 1400, Houston, TX 77027
(713) 624-4100

Honorable Leta Parks
247th Judicial District Court
1115 Congress Ave., Houston, TX 77002
(713) 755-6246

John D. Payne
440 Louisiana, Suite 850, Houston, TX 77002
(713) 225-6600

Maureen Peltier
952 Echo Ln., Suite 422, Houston, TX 77024
(713) 461-5288

Collaborative Lawyer Directory

Barbara Ramirez
550 Westcott, Suite 350, Houston, TX 77007
(713) 956-6565

Donald R. Royall
4550 Post Oak Place, Suite 341, Houston, TX 77027
(713) 462-6500

Barbara Runge
5615 Kirby Dr., Suite 920, Houston, TX 77005
(713) 523-5363

Elyssa Schnurr
Wilson & Associates, PC
2100 W. Loop South, Suite 1125, Houston, TX 77027
(713) 479-9700

Brenda Keen
1800 Bering Dr., Suite 690, Houston, TX 77057
(713) 972-1320

Chris A. Spofford
2930 Revere, Suite 301, Houston, TX 77098
(713) 526-2400

Harry L. Tindall
1300 Post Oak Blvd., Suite 2200, Houston, TX 77056
(713) 622-8733

Norma Levine Trusch
4550 Post Oak Place, Suite 341, Houston, TX 77027
(713) 961-0256

Teresa Waldrop
3816 W. Alabama, Suite 200, Houston, TX 77027
(713) 871-9377

Kay Whyburn
550 Westcott, Suite 350, Houston, TX 77007
(713) 223-1408

Ellen A. Yarrell
1900 St. James Pl., Suite 850, Houston, TX 77056
(713) 621-3332

Sam (Trey) Yates, III
5225 Katy Fewy, Suite 550, Houston, TX 77007
(713) 932-7177

Alvin L. Zimmerman
3040 Post Oak Blvd., Suite 1300, Houston, TX 77059
(713) 552-1234

Diane Zomper
4151 S.W. Freeway, Suite 770, Houston, TX 77027
(713) 960-9696

HURST

Stephen Brewer
Leach & Ames, Attorneys at Law, PC
460 Harwood Rd., Hurst, TX 76054
(817) 280-0811

Elaine Ryan
669 Airport Freeway, Suite 206, Hurst, TX 76053
(817) 545-3280

Collaborative Lawyer Directory

IRVING

Martin Kahn
320 Decker Dr., Irving, TX 75062
(972) 258-6602

KINGWOOD

Tamara Paul
1420 C. Stonehollow Dr., Kingwood, TX 77339
(281) 359-3700

MCALLEN

Martin Morris
Dale & Klein
6301 N. 10th, McAllen, TX 78504
(956) 687-8700

MCKINNEY

George M. Parker
Parker & Montgomery
121 S. Tennessee St., McKinney, TX 75069
(972) 562-2212

Diana L. Porter
112B N. Tennessee St., McKinney, TX 75069
(972) 562-0038

MIDLAND

David Lindemood
214 W. Texas Ave., Suite 811, Midland, TX 79701
(432) 620-9944

Gayle Shackleford
P.O. Box 3112, Midland, TX 79702

MT. PLEASANT

D'Ann Colley
Colley & Colley
806 N. Jefferson Ave., Mt. Pleasant, TX 75456
(903) 572-7712

Robert Rolston
405 W. 3rd St., Mt. Pleasant, TX 75455
(903) 577-0881

Kerry Dan Woodson
806 N. Jefferson, Mt. Pleasant, TX 75456
(903) 572-6675

NAVASOTA

Joe Falco, III
Falco & Falco
400 E. Washington Ave, #301, Navasota, TX 77868
(936) 825-6533

Collaborative Lawyer Directory

PLANO

Nancy Amick
2121 W. Spring Creek Pkwy., Suite 203, Plano, TX 75023
(214) 473-8383

Sharon Easley
Easley & Marquis
5000 Legacy Dr., Suite 400, Plano, TX 75024
(972) 578-9597

Jody L. Johnson
Allison & Johnson, LLP
5000 Legacy Dr., Suite 160, Plano, TX 75024
(972) 608-4300

Lisa Marquis
Easley & Marquis
5000 Legacy Dr., Suite 400, Plano, TX 75204
(972) 578-9597

Kathryn J. Murphy
Koons, Fuller, VandenEykel & Robertson
5700 W. Plano Pkwy, Suite 2200, Plano, TX 75093
(972) 769-2727

William J. Roberts
Gay, McCall, Isaacks, Gordon & Roberts
777 E. 15th St., Plano, TX 75074
(972) 424-8501

Carole K. Stevens
2121 W. Spring Creek Pkwy., Suite 203, Plano, TX 75023
(972) 473-8383

RICHMOND

Carolyn McDaniel
McDaniel & McMeans
303 S. 2nd St., Richmond, TX 77469
(281) 342-7766

ROCKWALL

Terese Easter
PMB 105
519 Interstate 30, Rockwall, TX 75087
(972) 772-7755

Susan Z. Wright
Alternative Resolution Associates, LLC
P.O. Box 1435, Rockwall, TX 75087
(972) 772-0285

ROUND ROCK

Patricia Brown
595 Round Rock West Dr., Suite 201,
Round Rock, TX 78681
(512) 246-1149

Lori Summers
1901 Palm Valley, Suite 110, Round Rock, TX 78664
(512) 244-6658

Collaborative Lawyer Directory

SAN ANTONIO

Michael D. Bowles
8400 Blanco Rd., Suite 205, San Antonio, TX 78216
(210) 377-0008

Clarence Bray
Bray & Chappell, Inc.
1250 N.E. Loop 410, Suite 315, San Antonio, TX 78209
(210) 828-2058

Solomon Casseb, III
Casseb & Pearl, Inc.
127 E. Travis St., San Antonio, TX 78205
(210) 223-4381

Ben R. Chappell
Bray & Chappell, Inc.
1250 N.E. Loop 410, Suite 315, San Antonio, TX 78209
(210) 828-2055

John Compere
Shaddox, Compere, Walraven & Good, PC
1250 N.E. Loop 410, Suite 725, San Antonio, TX 78209
(210) 822-2018

Kathleen Curry
8100 Broadway, Suite 102, San Antonio, TX 78209
(210) 225-4001

Shirley Ehrlich
9311 San Pedro, Suite 700, San Antonio, TX 78216
(210) 641-6707

Robert F. Estrada
8118 Datapoint Dr., San Antonio, TX 78229
(210) 614-6400

Amy A. Geistweidt
Higdon Hardy & Zuflacht, LLP
12000 Huebner Rd., Suite 200, San Antonio, TX 78230
(210) 349-9933

Sue M. Hall
222 Travis Park Plaza
711 Navarro, San Antonio, TX 78205
(210) 222-2333

Charles E. Hardy
Higdon Hardy & Zuflacht, LLP
12000 Huebner Rd., Suite 200, San Antonio, TX 78230
(210) 349-9933

James Higdon
Higdon Hardy & Zuflacht, LLP
12000 Huebner Rd., Suite 200, San Antonio, TX 78230
(210) 349-9933

Jo Chris Lopez
Shaddox, Compere, Walraven & Good, PC
1250 N.E. Loop 410, Suite 725, San Antonio, TX 78209
(210) 822-2018

Mark L. Medley
14350 Northbrook, No. 150, San Antonio, TX 78232
(210) 490-7999

Collaborative Lawyer Directory

Victor H. Negron, Jr.
750 E. Mulberry, Suite 510, San Antonio, TX 78212
(210) 738-8750

Jeffrey Pfeifer
1931 N.W. Military Hwy., Suite 215, San Antonio, TX 78213
(210) 308-5996

Robinson C. Ramsey
Soules & Wallace
100 W. Houston St., Suite 1500, San Antonio, TX 78205
(210) 224-9144

James D. Stewart
115 E. Travis St., Suite 1900, San Antonio, TX 78205
(210) 225-4321

Victoria Valerga
7300 Blanco Rd., Suite 103, San Antonio, TX 78216

F. Lynne Wilkerson
235 E. Mitchell St., San Antonio, TX 78210
(210) 531-1817

Patricia Wueste
800 N.W. Loop 410, Suite 414-S, San Antonio, TX 78216
(210) 349-1638

Harold C. Zuflacht
Higdon Hardy & Zuflacht, LLP
12000 Huebner Rd., Suite 200, San Antonio, TX 78230
(210) 349-9933

SUGAR LAND

Alice Klosowsky
14015 S.W. Freeway, Suite 14, Sugar Land, TX 77478
(281) 277-8998

Peter Sperling
20 Clansmoor Ct., Sugar Land, TX 77479

TEMPLE

David Greenfield
Blanks, Greenfield & Rhodes
220 N. Main, Temple, TX 76501
(254) 778-4181

THE WOODLANDS

Patrice McDonald
Schulze & McDonald, LLP
214 Nursery Rd., The Woodlands, TX 77380
(281) 363-0414

Ruth Vernier
2441 High Timbers, Suite 100, The Woodlands, TX 77380
(281) 364-1187

Elizabeth Woodward
1400 Woodloch Forest, Ste 120, The Woodlands, TX 77380
(281) 367-4685

TOMBALL

George M. Clifton
Clifton, Dodson & Sortino, LLP
14011 Park Dr., Suite 110, Tomball, TX 77375
(281) 351-4040

TYLER

Paul T. Fanning
400 Troup Hwy., Tyler, TX 75701
(903) 597-7878

WACO

Robin Baird
Montez, Williams & Baird, PC
3809 W. Waco Dr., Waco, TX 76710
(254) 759-8600

WEATHERFORD

Jerry Buckner
206 Houston, Weatherford, TX
(817) 594-5428

Gary Westenhover
101 S. Main, Weatherford, TX 76086
(817) 599-9451

Appendix A

Important Decisions in Your Divorce

1) Custody
    a) Sole managing conservator
    b) Possessory conservator
    c) Joint managing conservators
        i) Equal possession
        ii) Unequal possession
    d) Grandparent possessory conservator
2) Rights, responsibilities, privileges and duties
    a) Rights of parent at all times
    b) Rights and duties during possession
    c) Duty to provide information
    d) Right to establish primary residence
    e) Geographical restriction
    f) Right to consent to medical, dental and surgical treatment involving invasive procedures and to consent to psychiatric and psychological treatment
    g) Right to represent the child in legal action
    h) Right to consent to marriage and enlistment in armed forces
    i) Right to make decisions concerning child's education
    j) Right to services and earnings of child
    k) Right to act as agent of child's estate
    l) Right to receive child support
    m) Duty to pay child support
        i) Amount and term
        ii) Withholding order
        iii) Security
        iv) Charge against estate of obligor

3) Visitation/possession of children
- a) Weekdays
- b) Weekends
- c) Holiday
- d) Extended summer
- e) Other
- f) Terms of child pickup, delivery

4) Medical
- a) Premiums
- b) Uninsured medical expenses

5) Property division and distribution
- a) Real property
- b) Furniture, furnishings
- c) Personal effects
- d) Cash accounts
- e) Retirement
- f) Stock options
- g) Union benefits
- h) Insurance with surrender value
- i) Vehicles
- j) Stocks and bonds
- k) Businesses
- l) Contingent claims
- m) Debts

6) Taxes
- a) Payment/refund
- b) Preparation
- c) Exemptions

7) Miscellaneous
- a) Attorneys' fees
- b) Confirmation of separate property
- c) COBRA
- d) Name change

Appendix B

COLLABORATIVE LAW DISCLOSURE STATEMENT: MARRIAGE DISSOLUTION

Introduction

Should you choose to participate in the Collaborative Law model regarding your divorce, you and your spouse would each have an attorney, and all would have a shared commitment to avoid litigation. The Collaborative Law process primarily entails informal discussions and four-way conferences for purposes of settling all issues. Each party and his or her attorney agree to adhere to honesty and mutual respect for the Collaborative Law process. Both parties and counsel commit themselves to resolving differences justly and equitably without resort or threat of resort to court proceedings. Collaborative Law utilizes informal discovery, such as the voluntary exchange of financial information and the reliance on agreed upon neutral experts, such as tax advisors, financial planners, appraisers and family counselors. The parties may be assigned tasks to assist in preparing inventories and appraisals of assets and liabilities. Parenting plans, allocating parental responsibilities and time with their child(ren) are jointly worked out by the parents with the goal of serving the best interests of the family. The parties proceed in good faith to use their best efforts to arrive at solutions which address both parties' fundamental interests (needs, values, concerns, and priorities) and, if necessary, to compromise in order to reach a settlement of all issues that is acceptable to both parties. If the case cannot settle through the Collaborative Law process, the collaborative lawyers must withdraw and trial counsel may be retained.

Janet P. Brumley

Considerations When Deciding Whether to Participate in Collaborative Law

The following may be considered advantages to the Collaborative Law process:

Collaborative Law contemplates a series of two- or three-hour meetings (known as "four-way meetings") to allow for the gathering of needed information, to defuse any tension and to allow each side ample time to consider proposals. During these meetings, you will have the comfort of professional advice and guidance from your respective Collaborative Lawyers. In contrast, mediation involves sessions which can be lengthy marathons to conclusion, and some mediations are conducted without counsel present.

The Collaborative Law process preserves privacy by not airing differences in a public forum (the courthouse). Some of the agreement terms and most of the financial disclosures can be kept out of the public court record.

The parties retain control over the outcome when agreements are reached. Settlements to which both parties agree are more sustainable over long periods of time and invite more consistent compliance, than do court-ordered mandates with which neither party may be satisfied.

If the parties have children, the direct communication model of the Collaborative Law helps parties develop and preserve a cooperative relationship which will benefit those children as the parties go about the task of co-parenting during and post-divorce.

According to clinical research, the inevitable increase in hostility and conflict which comes out of adversarial litigation is known to emotionally damage litigants' children. The Collaborative Law process is designed to minimize post-divorce conflict.

Collaborative Law in Texas

There may be a benefit to you in increasing the chance that you and your spouse or your spouse's relatives and your mutual friends will continue to have positive relationships after the dissolution of your marriage.

You may not be the gambling type and would prefer not to take the risks inherent in court proceedings.

Collaborative Law can be more likely to level the playing field by having the parties agree at the outset that all legal fees will be drawn from community funds or will be otherwise allocated fairly.

Collaborative Law requires both lawyers and parties to explore solutions which address the interests of both parties, rather than take tactical positions to advantage one over the other.

Collaborative Law encourages creative solutions to meet your needs, which may differ from how the court would apply the law to the facts of the case.

Everyone has an economic incentive to work toward settlement — the parties because of the high cost of litigation; the lawyers because they would be forced to withdraw if settlement cannot be achieved.

The following could be considered disadvantages of the Collaborative Law process:

The disadvantage most often voiced is that it is less efficient to have two lawyers (the Collaborative Lawyer and then the Litigation Attorney), if the case is not settled. There may be some duplication of effort as the second lawyer catches up.

There are things that could have been done to prepare for trial that the time delay in getting started on trial preparation may make difficult or impossible — such as the discovery of certain relevant facts that are no longer accessible.

Court-ordered mechanisms to compel production of information will not be available during a Collaborative Law process.

A restraining order without prior notice to the other side could prevent unilateral disposition of property, incurring of debt or decisions concerning the child(ren), a remedy for which the Collaborative Law process does not offer.

You may agree to neutral experts during the Collaborative Law process and then not be able to use them if the case does not settle. You might need to hire and pay for additional experts to support your position in court.

The following are other considerations relating to the Collaborative Law process:

The Collaborative Law process is not appropriate when punitive action is sought, such as contempt proceedings to enforce prior orders.

The Collaborative Law process may not be appropriate if the necessary underlying honesty is lacking. If you believe your spouse is the type of person who would lie and/or would not be truthful in his/her dealings with you, the Collaborative Law process may not be appropriate for you. In the traditional litigation model, formal discovery may disclose concealed facts.

The Collaborative Law process prohibits taking tactical advantage of the other's mistakes, oversights and misinformation. In contrast, adversarial litigation allows litigants with the less meritorious case to prevail, in some instances, because of superior advocacy or technicalities unrelated to fairness and justice.

The Collaborative Law process, like mediation, may not be appropriate if there is a history or pattern of family violence. The court has remedies, such as protective orders, which are not utilized in the Collaborative Law process.

If you feel threatened or intimidated or feel like you are in an unequal bargaining position when you are in the presence of your spouse and do not feel that having your attorney present would help you overcome those feelings, the Collaborative Law process is not suitable for you.

No one who feels coerced into submitting to the Collaborative Law process should participate in that model.

If you require a public forum to vindicate and defend yourself from accusations of wrong-doing, the privacy of the Collaborative Law process may not be satisfying.

There may be a preliminary question of law or fact upon which all the negotiations depend that should be determined by the court at the outset.

Should the case not settle and the parties proceed to court, the court may not consider statements made in four-way meetings to be confidential, as they would be in mediation and other settlement conferences in the traditional litigation model. Thus, statements made by a party during a four-way meeting in the Collaborative Law process could possibly later be used against that party in court if the case did not settle.

If you value working toward a peaceful, amicable solution over winning at all costs, your values will be honored in the Collaborative Law process.

Appendix C

COLLABORATIVE LAW PARTICIPATION AGREEMENT: SEPARATION/MARRIAGE DISSOLUTION

PURPOSE

_____ and _____ (the "Parties") have chosen to use collaborative law procedures pursuant to Texas Family Code §6.603 and/or §153.0072 to settle the issues arising from the dissolution of their marriage. The primary goal of the collaborative law process is to settle all necessary issues of the parties' separation and dissolution of their marriage in a nonadversarial manner. The parties acknowledge the essence of the collaborative law process is the shared belief by participants that it is in the best interests of parties and their families in typical family law matters to commit themselves to avoiding litigation. The parties therefore adopt this conflict resolution process, which does not rely on a court-imposed resolution, but relies on an atmosphere of honesty, cooperation, integrity and professionalism geared toward the future well-being of the restructured family. The parties' goal is to avoid the negative economic, social and emotional consequences to the participants and their families associated with protracted litigation. The parties commit themselves to the collaborative family law process because the parties believe it to be a better way to resolve differences justly and equitably.

COMMITMENTS

The parties commit to a collaborative problem-solving process, which is:

A litigation free approach;
Based on the parties' empowerment and education;

Based on the development of the needs and interests of each party;

Based on all significant actions which affect participants' rights being taken only with the consent of all participants (no significant unilateral actions being taken);

Based on the parties taking responsibility for the decisions they make in resolving their differences; and

Based on the Collaborative Lawyers taking responsibility for assisting their respective clients to identify issues, gather and analyze all relevant information, develop options and understand their consequences, and to work through their own individual value conflicts, all of which is necessary to reach an acceptable, durable and maximized agreement.

UNDERSTANDINGS

Independent Representation

_____ is the Collaborative Lawyer for _____ , and _____ is the Collaborative Lawyer for _____(the "Collaborative Lawyers"). The parties understand that each Collaborative Lawyer is independent from the other and each represents his or her client only in the collaborative law process. The parties understand and agree that there is no privity of contract between one spouse and the other spouse's Collaborative Lawyer by virtue of this collaborative law process or this Participation Agreement. The parties understand that each Collaborative Lawyer is an advocate for his or her client only; no legal duty, by contract or otherwise, is owed by the other spouse's Collaborative Lawyer; and no attorney-client relationship exists between one spouse's Collaborative Lawyer and the other spouse by virtue of this Participation Agreement or the collaborative process.

Further, each party acknowledges that neither of them is an intended third-party beneficiary of any agreements made between the other party and his/her Collaborative Lawyer, and both parties acknowledge and agree that neither of them will rely on any representation by or opinion the Collaborative Lawyer for the other party, nor does the Collaborative Lawyer for the other party owe any duty of care to the party not represented by that Collaborative Lawyer. Each party is represented solely and exclusively by his/her own Collaborative Lawyer, and the participants' good faith undertakings set forth in this Agreement do not give rise under any circumstance to any claims, contractual or otherwise, by one party against the Collaborative Lawyer of the other party.

Court Involvement Only by Agreement

The parties agree and understand that as part of the collaborative process, the Collaborative Lawyers will not go to Court, other than to have Agreed Temporary Orders and/or an Agreed Final Decree entered, or to withdraw from a party's representation, if required. If the case cannot be settled on terms acceptable to the parties, or if either party seeks to file a motion in court or seek court intervention, both lawyers shall withdraw from the case. In that event, the parties may hire trial counsel to proceed with the case.

No Assurance of Settlement

The parties understand that there is no guarantee that the process will be successful in resolving the matter. They understand that the process cannot eliminate concerns about the differences that have led to the current conflict. They understand that they are each still expected to assert their own interests and their respective Collaborative Lawyers will help each of them to do so. The process, even with full and honest disclosure, will involve vigorous good-faith negotiation. Best efforts will be used to create proposals that meet the fundamental needs of both of the parties. The parties acknowledge that compromise may be needed in order to reach a settlement of all issues. Although the likely outcome of a litigated result may be discussed, the threat of litigation will not be used as a way of forcing settlement.

COMMUNICATION

The parties intend to effectively communicate with each other in order to efficiently and economically settle the dissolution of their marriage. Written and verbal communications will be respectful and constructive, and the parties will not make accusations or claims not based in fact.

It is agreed that communication during settlement meetings will be focused on the economic issues in the dissolution and issues relating to the child(ren) of the marriage and the constructive resolution of those issues. The parties and their lawyers understand that the costs for settlement meetings are substantial and require everyone's cooperation to make the best possible use of available resources. To achieve this goal, the parties agree not to engage in unnecessary discussions of past events.

The parties acknowledge that inappropriate communication regarding settlement of their divorce can be harmful to their child(ren). The parties agree that communication with any minor child(ren) regarding these issues will occur only as agreed by the parties. In resolving issues about sharing the enjoyment of and responsibility for the child(ren), the parties will make every effort to reach amicable solutions that promote the child(ren)'s best interests.

The parties agree to negotiate and resolve differences related to the child(ren) to promote a caring, loving, and involved relationship between the child(ren) and both parents. The parties agree not to seek a conservatorship evaluation while the matter is a collaborative case, unless the parties agree in writing otherwise. The parties agree to insulate the child(ren) from involvement in the disputes. Neither Collaborative Lawyer will interview the minor child(ren) unless both parties agree, and the child(ren)'s therapist or neutral child specialist, if any, approves. The parties will both attend a parent education course if required by the court or if either party requests such attendance.

To maintain an objective and constructive settlement process, the parties agree to discuss settlement of their dissolution issues only in the settlement conference setting, unless the parties agree to discussions outside of the conference setting. Settlement issues will not be discussed at unannounced times by telephone calls or appearances at the other party's residence or place of employment. The parties understand that, from time to time, the Collaborative Lawyers may meet or confer to plan agendas for settlement meetings and to draft or review documents, but no agreements will be made by the Collaborative Lawyers on behalf of the parties without their consent.

The parties will work to protect the respect and dignity of all involved, including parties, attorneys and consultants. The parties shall maintain a high standard of integrity and specifically shall not take advantage of each other or of what a party knows to be a miscalculation or inadvertent mistake of any other party and/or his/her Collaborative Lawyer, but instead, shall identify and correct any such known miscalculation or mistake.

NEUTRAL EXPERTS

When appropriate and needed, the parties will use neutral experts for purposes of valuation, cash flow analysis, and any other issue which requires expert advice and/or recommendations. The parties will agree in advance as to how the costs of the third party expert will be paid. Except upon the mutual written agreement of the parties to the contrary, any person or firm retained by either party or Collaborative Lawyer during the collaborative law process whose work product is used by either party or Collaborative Lawyer during the collaborative law process (other than material prepared for the benefit of the parties prior to the institution of this collaborative law process and unrelated to it, such as tax returns) is forever disqualified from appearing as a witness, expert or otherwise, for either party in any hearing or trial regarding the parties' marriage. All notes, work papers, summaries, opinions, and written or oral reports of these persons and/or firms shall be inadmissible as evidence in any legal proceeding involving the parties unless the parties agree in writing otherwise, but shall be furnished to successor counsel and/or any lawyer who renders a litigation opinion for either party, and shall be available for future settlement conferences, including, without limitation, mediation. The parties agree and consent that any neutral expert engaged in the collaborative process may communicate with any other lawyer retained by either party or with whom either party has consulted whether during or after termination of the collaborative law process.

The parties agree and consent that a neutral expert's opinion may be reviewed and considered by an expert retained in a future litigation process (whether a consulting or testifying expert). The litigation expert may, upon the written release of either party, with or without the other party's joinder, consult directly with the neutral expert. It is agreed that information received from the neutral expert may form the basis, in part, for a litigation expert's opinion, but such use does not constitute a waiver of the prohibition against any testimony, including without limitation, deposition testimony, of the neutral expert, unless the parties both agree in writing otherwise.

DISCLOSURE OF INFORMATION

The parties and the lawyers will deal with each other in good faith. The parties agree to promptly provide all necessary and reasonable information requested. The parties agree that the presumption is that a request for information is reasonable and will not be denied. However, the parties may negotiate the conditions under which information will be delivered or disclosed. Each party's request for information, questions and concerns will be respected and addressed in a reasonable and dignified atmosphere. The parties will be required to sign a sworn statement making full and fair disclosure of their income, assets and debts (a Sworn Inventory and Appraisement), unless they agree to waive such in writing.

The parties and their Collaborative Lawyers agree, pursuant to the collaborative law provisions of the Texas Family Code, to make full and candid exchange of information between the parties and their lawyers as necessary to make a proper evaluation of the case. The parties agree to make full disclosure of the nature, extent, value of — and all developments affecting — the parties' income, assets, and liabilities. The parties further agree to make full disclosure of all material information concerning the parties' child(ren). Refusal to be honest or failure to disclose such information shall be grounds for one or both Collaborative Lawyers' withdrawal from representation.

No formal discovery procedures will be used unless specifically agreed to in advance by the parties. The parties acknowledge that by using the collaborative law process, they are giving up the right during that process to have the Court compel the other party to participate in certain investigative procedures and methods that would be available to them in the litigation process.

The parties agree to maintain the confidentiality of any communication relating to the subject matter of the dispute made by the parties or their Collaborative Lawyers or other participants in the collaborative law procedure, whether before or after the institution of formal judicial proceedings. All meetings, communications, whether oral or written, and discussions involving any party, lawyer, or expert in the collaborative process are for settlement purposes only under Texas Rules of Evidence, Rule 408. The parties intend this confidentiality to cover all communications (written or oral) made during the collaborative law sessions, or between the Collaborative Lawyers or any experts with whom they or the parties consult in connection with this process, which are not memorialized in writing as binding agreements of the parties. They agree that such communication in the collaborative law procedure will not be subject to process requiring disclosure and that the communication will not be used as evidence against the participant in any judicial or administrative proceeding.

The parties agree that any record made in the collaborative law procedure is confidential and the participants will not be required to testify in any proceedings relating to or arising out of the matter in dispute concerning the confidential content of the collaborative law procedure. The parties agree that any oral communication or written material used in or made a part of the collaborative law procedure will only be admissible or discoverable if it is admissible or discoverable independent of the procedure. All communication made in the collaborative law procedure is for the purpose of promoting reconciliation, settlement and understanding only and is intended as settlement negotiations and discussions for which it would violate public policy to allow such to be used in evidence for or against either party. The parties agree that neither party shall seek to offer or compel testimony or production of documents created for the collaborative law procedure in any future legal proceedings, without the prior written consent and authorization of both parties. Unless the parties agree in writing otherwise, all matters, including the conduct and demeanor of the parties and their counsel during the settlement process, are confidential and may never be disclosed to anyone, including the court having jurisdiction over the matter, except that a party and/or his or her Collaborative Lawyer is free to disclose information to that party's successor Collaborative Lawyer or litigation counsel, and/or to any lawyer who renders a litigation opinion for that party.

ENFORCEABILITY OF AGREEMENTS

I. Temporary Agreements. In the event that the parties reach a temporary agreement for any purpose, the agreement may be put in writing by either party's lawyer and, if such an agreement is prepared, shall be signed by the parties and their Collaborative Lawyers, and if required by either party, shall be in the form of an Agreed Temporary Order and entered by the

Court. A Collaborative Lawyer shall be permitted to present to the Court a written agreement which is signed by both parties and the Collaborative Lawyers, for entry of a temporary order. The parties understand that if an agreement is not reduced to writing and signed by the parties and/or their respective Collaborative Lawyers, it will not be able to be enforced.

II.   Partial and Final Settlement Agreements. Any written agreement, whether partial or final, which is signed by both parties and their Collaborative Lawyers may be filed with the Court as a Collaborative Law Settlement Agreement in accordance with Texas Family Code §6.603 and §153.0072 and/or Rule 11 Agreement, which the Court may make retroactive to the date of the written agreement and which may be made the basis of a Court order. Should the case settle and the parties agree to divorce, the Collaborative Lawyers shall cooperate to prepare an Agreed Final Decree which contains the terms of the parties' agreements. Either or both Collaborative Lawyers shall be permitted to appear in Court to have the Agreed Final Decree entered.

III.   Withdrawal from the Collaborative Process. The parties understand and agree that neither Collaborative Lawyer shall be permitted to enforce any written agreements between the parties. Should the parties seek to enforce any written agreement over the objection of the other party, the parties must withdraw from the collaborative process. In such event, the Collaborative Lawyers shall withdraw as attorneys of record and, if required, shall consent to the substitution of trial counsel. If either party withdraws from the collaborative process, any written agreements between the parties and/or their attorneys made during the collaborative process, may be presented to the court as an agreement enforceable under Rule 11 of the Texas Rules of Civil Procedure and may become a court order, and either party would be entitled to judgment on a collaborative law settlement agreement if the agreement: (1) provides, in a prominently displayed statement that is boldfaced, capitalized, or underlined, that the agreement is not subject to revocation; and (2) is signed by each party to the agreement and the Collaborative Lawyer of each party.

LEGAL PROCESS

Court Proceedings: After this Collaborative Law Participation Agreement is signed by both parties and their Collaborative Lawyers, unless otherwise agreed or a withdrawal from the collaborative law process occurs (as set out hereafter) prior to reaching final agreement on all issues, no motion or document will be prepared or filed which would initiate court intervention, other than a Petition or Counter-Petition for Divorce and Answer, for which service of citation will be accepted by the parties' respective lawyers. No hearing shall be set thereon, other than a final hearing to enter an Agreed Decree. So long as the collaborative law procedures are in effect, there shall be no judicial intervention except to have the Court approve the settlement agreement, make the legal pronouncements, and sign the orders required by law to effectuate the agreement.

Withdrawal from Collaborative Law Process: If a party decides to withdraw from the collaborative law process, prompt written notice will be given to the other party through his or her lawyer, and joint notice of such termination, signed by the Collaborative Lawyers with or without joinder of both parties, shall be given to the Court. Upon withdrawal from the collaborative law process, there will be a thirty (30) day waiting period (unless there is an emergency) before any court hearing, to permit both parties to retain other lawyers and make an orderly transition. All temporary agreements will remain in full force and effect during this period. The intent of this provision is to avoid surprise and prejudice to the rights of the other party. It is mutually agreed that either party may bring this provision to the attention of the Court in requesting a postponement of a hearing.

Withdrawal of Counsel: If either party chooses to withdraw from the collaborative process by seeking Court involvement, both Collaborative Lawyers shall withdraw from the representation in accordance with Texas Family Code §§ 6.603 and/or 153.0072. Further, the parties understand that neither Collaborative Lawyer (nor any lawyer associated in the practice of law with him/her) may serve as litigation counsel in this case or in matters between the parties thereafter. The Collaborative Lawyers will cooperate in transferring copies of their respective files to their respective clients' successor counsel.

Either collaborative lawyer may withdraw unilaterally from the collaborative law process by giving three (3) days' written notice to his or her client and the other Collaborative Lawyer. Notice of withdrawal of a Collaborative Lawyer does not necessarily terminate the collaborative law process; however, in order for the process to continue, the party whose lawyer has withdrawn will need to retain a new Collaborative Lawyer who will agree in writing to be bound by this Participation Agreement.

Suspension of Court Intervention: The parties and their Collaborative Lawyers agree that Court intervention shall be suspended while the parties are using collaborative law procedures.

RIGHTS AND OBLIGATIONS PENDING SETTLEMENT

Although the parties have agreed to work outside the judicial system, the parties agree that neither party will:

1. Communicate with the other party in person, by telephone, or in writing in vulgar, profane, obscene, or indecent language or in a coarse or offensive manner.

Collaborative Law in Texas

2. Threaten the other party in person, by telephone, or in writing to take unlawful action against any person.

3. Place one or more telephone calls, anonymously, at an unreasonable hour, in an offensive and repetitious manner, or without a legitimate purpose of communication.

4. Cause bodily injury to the other party or a child of either party.

5. Threaten the other party or a child of either party with imminent bodily injury.

6. Destroy, remove, conceal, encumber, transfer, or otherwise harm or reduce the value of the property of one or both of the parties.

7. Falsify any writing or record relating to the property of either party.

8. Misrepresent or refuse to disclose to the other party, on proper request, the existence, amount, or location of any property of one or both of the parties.

9. Damage or destroy the tangible property of one or both of the parties, including any document that represents or embodies anything of value.

10. Tamper with the tangible property of one or both of the parties, including any document that represents or embodies anything of value, thereby causing pecuniary loss to the other party.

11. Sell, transfer, assign, mortgage, encumber, or in any other manner alienate any of the property of either party, whether personalty or realty, and whether separate or community, except as specifically agreed to in writing.

12. Incur any indebtedness, including but not limited to borrowing against any credit line or unreasonably using credit cards or cash advances against credit or bank cards, except as specifically agreed to in writing, or as specified in this agreement.

13. Make withdrawals from any checking or savings account in any financial institution for any purpose, except as specifically agreed to in writing, or as specified in this agreement.

14. Spend any sum of cash in the possession or subject to the control of either party for any purpose, except as specifically agreed to in writing, or as specified in this agreement.

15. Withdraw or borrow in any manner for any purpose from any retirement, profit-sharing, pension, death, or other employee benefit plan or employee savings plan or from any individual retirement account or Keogh account, except as specifically agreed to in writing.

16. Enter any safe-deposit box in the name of or subject to the control of either party, whether individually or jointly with others, unless the parties accompany each other and jointly enter the box for the sole purpose of inventorying or dividing its contents by mutual agreement.

17. Withdraw or borrow in any manner all or any part of the cash surrender value of life insurance policies on the life of either party, except as specifically agreed to in writing.

18. Change or in any manner alter the beneficiary designation on any pension, retirement plan or insurance policy, except as specifically agreed to in writing.

19. Cancel, alter, fail to renew or pay premium, permit to lapse or in any manner affect or reduce the value of the present level of coverage of any life, disability, casualty, automobile, or health insurance policies insuring the parties' property or persons, except as specifically agreed to in writing.

20. Change any provisions of any existing trust or will or execute a new trust or will without the prior written consent of the other party.

21.Terminate or in any manner affect the service of water, electricity, gas, telephone, cable television, or other contractual services, such as security, pest control, landscaping, or yard maintenance, at the residence of the other party or in any manner attempt to withdraw any deposits for service in connection with those services, except as specifically agreed to in writing.

22. Exclude the other party from the use and enjoyment of his or her respective residence.

23. Enter or remain on the premises of the residence of

the other party without the other's consent.

24. Open or divert mail addressed to the other party, except as specifically agreed to in writing.

25. Sign or endorse the other party's name on any negotiable instrument, check, or draft, such as tax refunds, insurance payments, and dividends, or attempt to negotiate any negotiable instrument payable to the parties or the other party without the personal signature of the other party.

26. Take any action to terminate or limit credit or charge cards in the name of the parties or the other party, except as specifically agreed to in writing.

27. Transfer balances between credit cards or open new accounts, except as agreed to in advance in writing.

28. Pay more than the outstanding balance owed on a credit card or charge account, except as specifically agreed to in writing.

29. Take any action to freeze or put a hold on any account with any financial institution from which the other party has the right to withdraw funds for purposes consistent with the authorizations contained in this agreement.

30. Enter, operate, or exercise control over the motor vehicles in the possession of the other party, except as specifically agreed to by the parties.

31. Discontinue or reduce the withholding for federal income taxes on either party's wages or salary, except as specifically agreed to in writing.

32. Destroy, dispose of, or alter any financial records of the parties, including but not limited to records from financial institutions (including canceled checks and deposit slips), all records of credit purchases or cash advances, tax returns, and financial statements.

33. Destroy, dispose of, or alter any e-mail or other electronic data, whether stored on a hard drive or on a diskette or other electronic storage device.

34. Institute any action in any other county, state, or nation attempting to obtain temporary or permanent orders concerning the marriage relationship of the parties, the dissolution of

that relationship, spousal support, the conservatorship and support of the child(ren) of the parties or any other issue incident to a divorce proceeding or other proceeding involving the marital or parent-child relationship, if applicable.

35. Exercise any stock options and warrants except as specifically authorized in advance by written agreement of the parties.

36. Exercise any general or limited power of attorney, whether or not recorded, granted to the other party by _____.

37. Pay any indebtedness owed by the parties or either of them prior to the date the indebtedness is due, unless agreed to specifically in writing by the parties.

38. Create or contribute to, or reduce the value or withdraw from or terminate, any trust of any kind or nature except as specifically authorized in advance by written agreement of the parties.

39. Make any gift of any kind or nature, other than usual and customary gifts to family members of either party or mutual friends or their child(ren).

40. Create or contribute to any uniform gifts/transfers to minor act accounts or any trust of any kind or nature, except as specifically agreed to in advance in writing by the parties.

41. File any extension or form with the Internal Revenue Service with regard to Federal Tax liability for any years of the marriage that limits the other party's choice of filing status, unless agreed to in advance in writing by the parties.

42. File any Federal Income Tax Return or amendment to any Federal Income Tax Return for any year of the marriage during the pendency of the matter without first providing a true and correct copy of such proposed return to the attorney of record for the other party at least 14 days in advance of the proposed tender to the Internal Revenue Service. This shall apply whether or not such filing is proposed to be by electronic methods or hard copy filing.

43. Change the locks, key mechanisms, dead bolts, security code, or otherwise restrict access to the parties' vacation

home located at _____, (but the parties are allowed to change the locks, key mechanisms, dead bolts, security codes and otherwise restrict access to their respective primary residences.)

44. Disturb the peace of the child(ren) of the marriage.

45. Remove the child(ren) of the marriage beyond the jurisdiction of the Court, acting directly or in concert with others, except by agreement of the parties.

46. Disrupt or remove the child(ren) of the marriage from the school or daycare facility where the child(ren) may be presently enrolled.

47. Hide or secrete the child(ren) of the marriage from the other party.

48. Refuse any child permission to speak telephonically with the other party or interrupt or listen in on any child's telephonic conversations with the other party.

Either party may:

1. Make expenditures and incur indebtedness for reasonable and necessary living expenses for food, clothing, shelter, transportation, education, ordinary and customary entertainment and travel, and medical care.

2. Make expenditures and incur indebtedness for reasonable lawyer's fees and expenses in connection with this separation/marriage dissolution.

3. Make withdrawals from accounts in financial institutions only for the purposes authorized by this agreement.

4. Engage in acts, make expenditures, incur indebtedness, make investments, and acquire, sell and transfer assets, as is reasonable and necessary to the conduct of either party's usual investment activities, business and occupation, subject to all such activities being fully disclosed and accounted for to the other party.

The parties agree that, upon the filing of an Original Petition for Divorce, either party may require that the other party sign an agreed temporary mutual injunction which includes the foregoing Rights and Obligations Pending Settlement to be entered by the Court. However, in the absence of such a Court Order, this Agreement shall nevertheless remain enforceable as a contract between the parties and may be the basis for a claim against the party violating its terms.

SCHEDULING

The parties agree that there will be scheduled at least two more 4-way sessions prior to mediation of this matter so long as the collaborative law process is ongoing. In furtherance of the collaborative law process. the parties agree to attempt to resolve unresolved issues with _____, as a mediator, or with another agreed upon mediator on or before _____, 20___, or on or before such other date as the parties may hereafter agree.

ATTORNEYS' FEES

The parties and their lawyers agree that the Collaborative Lawyers are entitled to be paid a reasonable fee for their services. The parties agree to make funds available from their community or separate estates, as needed, to pay both lawyers' fees. The parties understand that, if necessary, one party may be asked to pay both attorneys' fees from community property managed solely by him or her (i.e., his or her salary) or from separate funds. The parties agree that all attorneys' fees and costs (including expert fees) incurred by both parties shall be paid in full prior to entry of an agreed final decree of divorce.

ACKNOWLEDGMENT

Both parties and the Collaborative Lawyers acknowledge that they have read this Agreement, understand its terms and conditions, and agree to abide by them. The parties understand that by agreeing to this alternative method of resolving their dissolution issues, they are waiving certain rights, including the right to formal discovery (other than Sworn Inventories and Appraisements), formal court hearings, and other procedures provided by the adversarial legal system, unless they choose to withdraw from the process. The parties have chosen the collaborative law process to reduce emotional and financial costs, and to generate a final agreement that addresses their interests. The parties and their counsel agree to use their best efforts and make a good faith attempt to resolve their dissolution of marriage dispute, and/or the suit affecting the parent-child relationship suit, if applicable, on an agreed basis, without resorting to judicial intervention, except as provided herein. BOTH PARTIES AND THEIR RESPECTIVE COLLABORATIVE LAWYERS HEREBY PLEDGE TO COMPLY WITH AND TO PROMOTE THE SPIRIT AND LETTER OF THIS AGREEMENT, UNTIL AND UNLESS MODIFIED BY WRITTEN AGREEMENT SIGNED BY BOTH PARTIES AND THEIR RESPECTIVE COLLABORATIVE LAWYERS.

Dated: _____ Dated: _____

_____ _____

_____ _____

_____, _____,

Collaborative   Collaborative
Lawyer for   Lawyer for

Provided courtesy of the Dallas Alliance of Collaborative Family Lawyers

Appendix D

Documents That May Be Requested in Collaborative Law

Income Tax Returns. Personal, corporate, partnerships, joint ventures or other income tax returns, state and federal, including W-2, 1099 and K-1 forms.

Personal Property Tax Returns filed in this state or elsewhere at any time during the marriage.

Banking Information. All monthly bank statements for personal and business accounts, certificates of deposit, money market accounts in your possession or control from banks, savings and loan institutions, credit unions or other institutions.

Financial Statements. Submitted to banks, lending institutions, or any persons or entities.

Loan Applications. For all loans applied for, whether approved or not, for the last five years.

Broker's Statements. All statements of securities and commodities dealers and mutual funds maintained and received during the marriage and held individually, jointly, or as a trustee or guardian.

Stocks, Bonds and Mutual Funds. Certificates held individually, jointly, or as a trustee or guardian, including any stock brokerage accounts (and statements) owned during the marriage.

Stock Options. All records pertaining to stock options held in any corporate or other entity, exercised or not.

Pension, Profit Sharing, Deferred Compensation Agreement and Retirement Plans or any other kind of plan in which you are or have been a participant during the marriage.

Wills and Trust Agreements. Executed by you or your spouse, or in which either of you have a present or contingent interest or in which you are named a beneficiary or trustee.

Life Insurance. Or certificates of life insurance currently in existence, in which you or your spouse are named as either owner, or primary or contingent beneficiary, including any disability insurance currently in existence.

Outstanding Debts. Documents reflecting all debts owed, secured or unsecured, including personal loans and lawsuits now pending or previously filed in any court, showing the name of the debtor and/or creditors, the date each debt was incurred, the total amount and the unpaid balance.

Real Property. All deeds, closing statements, tax bills, appraisals, mortgages, security agreements, leases and other evidence (including monthly payments and present principal and interest balances) of any type of interest or ownership, whether as owner, co-owner, fiduciary, trust beneficiary (vested or contingent), partner, limited partner, shareholder joint venturer, mortgagee, developer, manager or otherwise during the term of the marriage, together with evidence of all contributions, in cash or otherwise, made by you or on your spouse's behalf, toward the acquisition of such real estate during the marriage or afterward.

Sale and Option Agreements on any real estate owned by either of you, either individually, through another person or entity, jointly, or as a trustee or guardian.

Motor Vehicles. Titles to all motor vehicles owned by you or your spouse, individually or jointly, at any time during the last five years, including airplanes, boats, automobiles or any other type of motor vehicle.

Corporate Interest. All records indicating any kind of personal interest in any corporation (foreign or domestic) or any other entities not evidenced by certificates or other instruments.

Partnership and Joint Venture Agreements to which you or your spouse have been parties during the marriage.

Employment Records. During the term of the marriage, showing evidence of wages, salaries, bonuses, commissions, raises, propositions, expense accounts and other benefits of deductions of any kind that were, are or may be paid, available, credited or withheld for any purpose by any individual or entity or to which you or your spouse were, are or may be, entitled in the future.

Memberships. Documents identifying participation rights in any country clubs, key clubs, private clubs, associations or fraternal organizations during the marriage, together with all monthly statements.

Gifts. All records pertaining to gifts of any kind made to you or by you to any person or entity, together with all records in connection with the transfer of personal property, by sale, gift or otherwise, during the marriage.

Inventory of Safe Deposit Boxes of you and your spouse.

Payroll Statements and Pay Stubs.

Financial Statements. All financial statements, profit and loss statements, balance sheets, income and expense statements, and operating statements regarding the parties and prepared by or on behalf of the parties.

Articles of Incorporation or Organization. All articles of incorporation or organization of any entity in which the parties now claim or have claimed any legal or equitable interest.

Insurance Policies. All policies of insurance, whether health, automobile, disability, casualty, homeowner's personal articles or otherwise, in which the parties claim any insurance protection.

Mortgages/Accounts Receivable. All mortgages, notes receivable, accounts receivable, or other evidence or information pertaining to debts due in which you own or claim any interest, whether payable to you or your spouse individually or otherwise.

Lines of Credit/Loans. Copies or originals of all credit files, loan files, loan, credit or lease applications, promissory notes, guaranty agreements, lease agreements, lines of credit, contracts for drafting authority, security agreements or other obligations and contractual agreements.

Psychological/Psychiatric Records. All records, including invoices, relating to medical, psychological and psychiatric treatments, consultations or diagnoses of the parties.

Telephone Records. All telephone records, including residence, business, cellular and portable telephone phones.

Transfers to a Third Party. Every document relating to any money or property that has been used or expended for the use and benefit of any party other than your spouse, regardless of whether you claim such money or property was used or expended for business purposes or adequate consideration was given.

Instruments of Guarantee. Every document that personally guaranteed the indebtedness of any other person or corporation, regardless of whether the guaranty is presently in effect.

Power of Attorney. Each power of attorney granted by either of you.

Pawn Tickets. All documents relating to any items of personal property pawned, sold or consigned to a pawn shop or other similar entity or individual, or used as collateral for a loan at a pawn or loan company.

Records of Cash Documents or Transactions. Records of purchases of traveler's checks, money orders, cashier's checks, or other documents evidencing a cash transaction to which you were a party.

Documents Relating to Separate Property Interest. Documents pertaining to the acquisition of property (a) owned prior to your marriage; (b) acquired during the marriage by gift, descent or devise; and/or (c) during the marriage by any expenditure of separate funds, or right of reimbursement claimed by either of you with respect to any community property owned or claimed by either of you.

Other Lawsuits. Documents including all pleadings, correspondence, reports, discovery documents, agreements, releases, judgments, etc. relating to each and every lawsuit, other than this lawsuit, to which either of you has been a party.

Personalty Instruments. Bills of sale, payment or receipt records, title certificates, invoices, receipts, inventories and lists, and any and all other instruments relating to the ownership of all personal property including the following items of personalty: coin collection; stamp collection; photographic equipment; household furniture, furnishings, appliances and fixtures; tools; automobiles; aircraft; trucks, trailers; boats and motors; recreational vehicles; animals of each and every type, except household pets; stocks and bonds and other securities; television, video tape and radio equipment and materials, including tapes, disks, records and cassettes; insurance policies; jewelry, electronic and/or electronic communication equipment and materials; firearms; hunting and fishing equipment; office equipment and materials; cash proceeds; and books, vases, and art objects.

Frequent Flyer Mileage Accounts. All books, records, documents and instruments pertaining to frequent flyer mileage accounts received by either of you from any source.

Prior Court Orders. All court orders requiring either of you to pay or entitling either of you to receive spousal maintenance, alimony or child support.

Provided courtesy of the Dallas Alliance of Collaborative Family Lawyers

Appendix E

Agenda for First Four-Way Meeting

Introductions and Background of Participants
If the participants have not all met and do not all know each other, make introductions by having the participants tell those with whom they are unfamiliar some background information about themselves (in an order that feels most comfortable to all).

Review the collaborative law participation agreement together and make any agreed changes.

Sign agreement.

Sign the e-mail authorization.

Schedule three or four future four-way meetings.

Discuss expectations of conduct and read aloud, if requested.

Discuss laminated process anchors.

Explain the road map to resolution using collaborative law process.

Discuss focusing on interests in the collaborative process document.

Explain the problem-solving method of the collaborative process:
- Understanding interests
- Gathering information
- Developing options
- Evaluating options
- Negotiating best possible outcome

Normalize difficulties in conflict resolution.

Identify parties' common goals, interests and concerns and

begin to identify individual interests (needs, goals, values, desires, fears, concerns and priorities).

Discuss immediate issues:

• If no court action has been filed, decide if and when it will be commenced, and by whom.

• If court action has or will be commenced, sign the notice of collaborative law procedures.

• Discuss the option of agreed temporary orders setting forth mutual injunctions during the pendency of the matter.

• Discuss any pressing concerns/issues that require immediate attention.

Identify what issues each party wants to address at future meetings in order to have a final resolution.

Discuss the option of engaging neutral experts.

Discuss the source of funds to pay for legal and neutral expert fees in an equitable manner.

Discuss plan for gathering information, including preparation of income and expense forms and inventories, if applicable.

Plan the agenda for the next four-way meeting:

• Create a list of assignments for all participants.

• Ask and answer any questions.

Provided courtesy of the Dallas Alliance of Collaborative Family Lawyers

Appendix F

Process Anchors
(HINTS TO REMEMBER
AT 4-WAY SESSIONS)

RECOGNIZE THE FUTILITY OF ARGUING:

- Identify your own perspectives, interests, beliefs.
- Listen for those of the other person.
- Arguing is a waste of time.

BE EFFECTIVE:

- Ask yourself if your conduct is helping you meet your interests.
- Is what you are doing moving you closer to your shared goals?

IF YOU HAVE A COMPLAINT, RAISE IT AS YOUR CONCERN AND FOLLOW IT UP WITH A CONSTRUCTIVE SUGGESTION AS TO HOW IT MIGHT BE RESOLVED.

AVOID LANGUAGE THAT IS CRITICAL, JUDGMENTAL, ACCUSATORY, BLAME-ORIENTED, SARCASTIC OR INFLAMMATORY.

COMMIT TO THE FULLEST DEVELOPMENT OF CHOICES AND ALTERNATIVES.

BE READY TO WORK FOR WHAT YOU BELIEVE IS THE MOST CONSTRUCTIVE AND ACCEPTABLE AGREEMENT FOR BOTH OF YOU AND YOUR FAMILY.

TAKE RESPONSIBIILITY FOR YOUR CHOICES.

Appendix G

Road Map to Resolution
Using Collaborative Law Process (Generic)

I. Understanding and agreeing to the process
    A. Reviewing and signing collaborative agreement
    B. Reviewing and agreeing to ground rules
    C. Discussing and setting up additional protocols
       or ground rules
II. Discussing Interests and Goals
    A. Preparing for discussion of interests and goals
       1. Reviewing summary information
       2. Reading material
       3. Preparing with each collaborative lawyer
       4. Determining time and place
    B. Meeting to discuss interests and goals
       at first four-way meeting
III. Dealing with Any Interim Issues
IV. Gathering Information
    A. Deciding which information is requested
       to be shared
    B. Providing and reviewing requested information
    C. Reviewing shared information to reach consensus
       and identify differences
       1. Work through differences
       2. Gather additional information if needed
       3. Reach compromises for settlement
          purposes
V. Generating possible resolutions
    A. Preparing for presenting possible resolutions
       1. Summarizing information gathered
       2. Preparing with one's own
          collaborative lawyer

    3. Determining time and place for discussion
    4. Brainstorming possible resolutions (as
       many options and alternatives as can be
       creatively generated) – anything goes
VI. Reaching Agreement
    A. Beginning to analyze the "brainstorming possible
       resolutions" in the context of each party's
       interests and goals
    B. Evaluate the consequences of choosing the
       various possible resolutions
    C. Eliminate resolution ideas which do not
       sufficiently meet important goals of either party
    D. Narrow the resolution ideas to those which meet
       the most of both parties' interests
    E. Finalize the agreement to yield the best
       possible outcome with the lawyers' input as
       to legal considerations

Provided courtesy of the Dallas Alliance of Collaborative Family Lawyers

NOTES:

NOTES:

NOTES: